MAKE IT A GREAT DAY

How to Feel Awesome So That You Can Help Others

Jarrett Robertson

MAKE IT A GREAT DAY: How to Feel Awesome So That You Can Help Others
www.makeitagreatday.ca
Copyright © 2021 Jarrett Robertson

ISBN: 978-1-77277-408-5

All rights reserved. No portion of this book may be reproduced mechanically, electronically, or by any other means, including photocopying, without permission of the publisher or author except in the case of brief quotations embodied in critical articles and reviews. It is illegal to copy this book, post it to a website, or distribute it by any other means without permission from the publisher or author.

Limits of Liability and Disclaimer of Warranty
The author and publisher shall not be liable for your misuse of the enclosed material. This book is strictly for informational and educational purposes only.

Warning – Disclaimer
The purpose of this book is to educate and entertain. The author and/or publisher do not guarantee that anyone following these techniques, suggestions, tips, ideas, or strategies will become successful. The author and/or publisher shall have neither liability nor responsibility to anyone with respect to any loss or damage caused, or alleged to be caused, directly or indirectly by the information contained in this book.

Medical Disclaimer
The medical or health information in this book is provided as an information resource only, and is not to be used or relied on for any diagnostic or treatment purposes. This information is not intended to be patient education, does not create any patient-physician relationship, and should not be used as a substitute for professional diagnosis and treatment.

Self-Publishing

Printed in Canada and the United States of America

Table of Contents

Dedication vii
About the Author viii
Acknowledgements xi
Foreword xiii

Part I – You **1**

Chapter 1: Project #4 .... **3**
Laugh 3
Consistency 6
Water 7
No Elevators and Park Far Away 9
Eat Cake in the Morning 11
As Hard as You Can Go 12

Chapter 2: Chemical Reaction **15**
Tell Me More 15
Dopamine 23
Endorphins 25
Serotonin 25
Oxytocin 26
Cortisol 27

Chapter 3: In a Day **31**
News 31
Schedule 34
Social Media 36
Sleep 39
Work 42
Phone a Friend 44

Chapter 4: Take Control ... 47
Amygdala Hijacking ... 47
Fear ... 49
Music ... 50
Thoughts ... 53
Relationships ... 55

Chapter 5: Emotional Drivers ... 59
Need for Certainty ... 59
Need for Variety ... 60
Need for Significance ... 61
Need for Connection ... 62
Need for Growth ... 64
Need for Contribution ... 65

Part II – Emotional Intelligence ... 69

Chapter 6: Emotional Intelligence ... 71
What Is EI? ... 71
Why EI Is More Important Than IQ ... 73
Test Your Emotional Intelligence ... 75
Interpersonal Skills Self-Assessment ... 76
The Maetrix EI Test ... 77
Harvard Business Review (HBR) ... 77

Chapter 7: Leaders ... 79
How to Develop EI for Leaders ... 80
Self-Awareness ... 81
Self-Regulation ... 81
Motivation ... 81
Empathy ... 81
Social Skills ... 82

Chapter 8: Sales 93
Concepts to Increase Sales 93
Self-Awareness 95
Self-Regulation 96
Motivation 96
Empathy 97
Social Skills 97

I dedicate this book to you!
If you are reading this, you are the person this is meant for.
If you are looking for ways to be your best every day
and feel amazing, I want you to know that you absolutely can.
There is no, one, right way; there is just your way.
I'm motivated every day to help people believe.
Thank you for who you are.

About the Author

At first glance, you might see a polished speaker, a financial expert, and a successful author. But peel back the layers, and you'll find a story of relentless resilience, unwavering determination, and an indomitable spirit that has triumphed against all odds.

Jarrett's journey began with a dream that seemed destined to shatter. Accepted into Brown University on a Division 1 hockey scholarship, he soared with anticipation. However, by 2003, the harsh reality hit hard— he was forced to take a year off due to academic struggles, a devastating blow that shook the very foundation of his aspirations.

But where others might have faltered, Jarrett found the strength to rise. Returning to Brown in 2004, he seized his second chance with a ferocity born from adversity. Graduating in 2006 with a degree in Human Development marked not just an academic achievement but a testament to resilience—a monumental comeback from the brink of defeat.

Yet, his journey was far from over. For three years, he lived the grueling life of a semi-pro hockey player, battling debt and uncertainty. But with each setback, he refused to yield. Life, however, seldom adheres to a linear trajectory. At 29, stranded at a Pennsylvania gas station with no means to continue the journey, the specter of adversity loomed large. Yet, it is in the crucible of such moments that resilience finds its voice.

Transitioning into the fitness industry in 2010, he forged a new path as a male physique competitor, defying odds and clinching victories in a realm where discipline and dedication reign supreme. Sponsored by leading supplement companies, and featured in prestigious fitness publications, perhaps this was a turning point, but life had more challenges in store.

Simultaneously in 2010, Jarrett entered the financial services industry, facing the daunting task of building a practice from scratch despite a lack of financial expertise and a history of poor decisions. Yet, he embraced the challenge head-on, driven by a desire to help others secure their financial well-being.

Jarrett faced the abyss and emerged stronger each time. Navigating the tumultuous currents of personal struggles— confronting familial trauma and alcoholism to grappling with the shadow of mental and emotional damage—instilled within him, an unwavering resolve to confront life's challenges head-on.

Yet, amid the chaos of life, and over 25 relocations his narrative is one of relentless pursuit, anchored in the belief that adversity is not an impediment but a catalyst for growth.

In 2016, he ascended to executive leadership within one of Canada's premier financial institutions, leveraging his experiences to shape a narrative of empathy, perseverance, and authentic leadership. The accolades that followed—earning the prestigious CFP® designation, becoming an Executive Circle member of the Financial Psychology Institute, a Psychology of Financial Planning Specialist, and being ordained as an officiant—serve as milestones in a journey marked by tenacity and fortitude.

In 2021, on the cusp of his 40th birthday, Jarrett penned his inaugural book, "Make It A Great Day," a testament to the transformative power of optimism in the face of adversity. But perhaps the pinnacle of his journey and subsequent collaborations came in 2024, with luminaries such as FBI Negotiator Chris Voss and esteemed colleague Michael Laughlin culminated in the publication of "Empathetic Leadership" and "Untapped 60," amplifying the message of resilience and perseverance to a global audience. These collaborations encapsulate the essence of his journey— forging connections, overcoming obstacles, and finding strength in vulnerability.

Through every twist and turn, he has embraced life's challenges with a smile, determined to find solutions and appreciate the journey. His story is not just one of success but of resilience, perseverance, and the unwavering belief that no dream is too big to conquer. As a speaker, Jarrett brings not just expertise but a lived experience that inspires others to embrace their journey and make every day a great one.

Make It a Great Day

Jarrett is available for live keynote presentations.
For more information, please visit **www.untapped60.com**

Acknowledgements

To Locker (Mike Laughlin): This is finally the time for me to tell you that, because of the difference in our age, I know you have always looked up to me as a big brother. Very few people will know someone in their lifetime who has faced the decision to choose life over death. You have done this twice. Your stories are seared within me and are the single biggest reason why I will always move forward. Thank you for being my inspiration. Because of you, I will never fail.

Twenty-two years and counting, and my day is immediately better the instant I hear, "Johnny." Manner (Chris Mann), you are a big bro, best friend, teammate, and most importantly, a confidant. You have worked so hard your entire life and are someone I strive to emulate on so many levels. You see and hear the worst on a daily basis but always make sure to make other people smile. Thank you for always being there for me, and for being who you are.

Krusto (Chris Runions): You and I met in grade 4 and have been best friends ever since. You were my best man in my wedding, and I'm pretty sure I had you penciled in since the 9th grade. No matter what happens in a day, I can count on a call from you that will last 90 seconds or span 45 minutes, and I look forward to those calls every day. You are one of the greatest people I have ever known, Krusto; and simply put, the world needs more people like you.

Make It a Great Day

Hudson, you are my boy; and Benton, you are my little man. People always said to have kids and that it is the greatest thing in theworld. Gentlemen, you challenge me every day and make me a betterman; thank you. You are both so kind and have hearts as big as the moon. You are creative in your own ways and are both extremely driven. It is inspiring to watch you grow; thank you. I intend and promise to be there every day of your lives. I will push you, I will hold you, I will watch you fail, I will watch you learn, and I will watch you win—I will love you every single day, and I am so proud of you. When I am no longer here, always remember, fellas: "When you fall down...."

To my sister, Mandy Cox. What a ride we have been on—wow! Let me tell you that although I'll never remember the things that you did for me throughout our childhood, I truly believe we are as close as we are for a reason. I am where I am because I have you, not only as a sister but as my biggest fan. In every situation I am in, I picture you behind me, glaring down my opponent and saying, "You better listen; this is my brother!" Thank you. You are my big sister and always will be. Love you!

"If we are going to get married, we should probably have each other's numbers." They say that when you know, you know. Lacey, I owe you a lifetime of thank you's and appreciation for coming into and being a part of my life. Together, we have created life and built the most incredible, loving, and sincere family. You are the rock of our family, and the constant that we can all count on every single day. Your patience, understanding, and support are everything I have ever dreamed of and need. I am a better man because of you, and I am where I am in my life because of your unconditional love. I meant it when I said "you are the only one I want to figure out this thing called life with." I intend and promise to love you forever. You are my love. OMWH

Foreword

Michael D.N Laughlin – 3-time trauma survivor
"Jarrett has truly been a game-changer in my life. Whenever I'm having a tough day, I am so thankful that I can pick up the phone and call him. His contagious positivity and inspiring words never fail to lift my spirits and turn my day around. His platform, Make It A Great Day, is a treasure trove of uplifting content and guidance, encouraging us all to embrace every day with a positive mindset. I'm immensely proud of my friend and the incredible community he's built. If you're seeking a daily dose of motivation, joy, encouragement, support, courses and tools that will help you thrive, I wholeheartedly recommend following Jarrett and Make It A Great Day. Your smile will thank you"

K.Daize - Director, Springrocc Wealth & Estate Inc
"I have known Jarrett for a long time and have watched him bring Make It A Great Day to life. The best way I can describe it to you is that it is the 'The positivity you didn't know you needed'. His passion for spreading motivation and empowering individuals is truly remarkable. Jarrett, the driving force behind Make It A Great Day and Untapped 60, is a beacon of inspiration. His vision has crafted a sanctuary of encouragement, providing the kind of uplifting energy we all crave. His dedication to helping us see the brighter side of life is genuine, and it resonates through every aspect of this platform. Make It A Great Day is a must for those seeking motivation, guidance, and a community that genuinely cares. The personalized messages, insightful content, and the incredible sense of belonging that his platform offers make it a haven of positivity. It's a place where your spirit is lifted, your goals are nurtured, and your confidence is boosted. Make It A Great Day is an investment in yourself and your well-being. It's an affirmation that you are ready to embrace a more positive outlook on life. Don't miss out on this chance to enhance your days and fuel your journey with inspiration."

www.makeitagreatday.ca

"Don't be pushed by your problems,
be led by your dreams"
~Ralph Waldo Emerson

Part I – You

Chapter 1

Project #4

Laugh

Make Yourself Laugh

Next time you're in the car or somewhere by yourself, try laughing. You don't have to think of anything funny; just start laughing. If you do it a few times, you will actually start laughing at yourself, and by getting to this point, you release feel-good brain chemicals. Until now, scientists haven't proven that like exercise and other activities, laughing causes a release of so-called endorphins.

If making yourself laugh is tough, find a video on YouTube or carry a picture with you that makes you laugh. I've been known to fall into the YouTube rabbit hole by watching AGT's funniest auditions, or outtakes from movies that I have watched. Other hilarious videos are dogs (or other animals) who fail at being dogs.

By laughing before you start your day, your workout, a meeting, an activity, or whatever it may be, you're setting yourself up to feel awesome (proven by science). Like so many other things that I discuss, I really try to provide the "why" behind it all, so that it (hopefully) makes more sense for you.

Short-term Benefits

Laughing stimulates your organs. Laughter enhances your intake of oxygen-rich air; stimulates your heart, lungs, and muscles; and increases the endorphins that are released by your brain. Think about the person that you run into who has just finished laughing. You immediately know and ask (or say), "Wow, you're in a good mood," or "What's so funny?" And chances are, you smile right along with them. It's contagious!

Laughing Will Soothe Tension

As you laugh and you increase the oxygen-rich air available to your body, it also will stimulate circulation and aid muscle relaxation, both of which help reduce some of the physical symptoms of stress. Think about when you're tensed up because of something someone said or did or didn't do (maybe your kids, your spouse, a colleague, an opponent, or a teammate). Your hands might be clenched, you feel that tension in your shoulders, and maybe your face is starting to heat up. Then someone or something makes you laugh because, in all reality, it's not that big of a deal, and you immediately feel this release come over you. I'm not suggesting that your emotional response is not accurate and that it will go away; what I'm suggesting is that it is a way for you to "take a deep breath" so that you can ease the tension.

Long-term Effects

Laughing can improve your immune system; how incredible is that? Negative thoughts manifest into chemical reactions that can affect your body by bringing more stress into your system and decreasing your immunity. You may not think the news has an effect on you, but guess what? It does.

In contrast, positive thoughts actually release neuropeptides that help fight stress and potentially more-serious illnesses. Watch things, listen to things, and do things that you like and that make you laugh. It's healthy!

Relieve Pain

Laughter may ease pain by causing the body to produce its own natural painkillers. When a child hurts themselves, what does every parent try to do? First, they console them to make sure they are not seriously injured, but I think of my two turbo boys who, daily, hurt themselves. At this point, if I hear a cry, I know they are fine, and I really have no reaction anymore (I know, I know… father of the year!). In reality, I make sure they are okay, and I immediately ask how tough they are and for them to show me their muscles. If I get no reaction, I take it a step further and tell them that we have to call our doctor, who will come over and cut off their nose for them so that it does not hurt anymore. I do this with an uplifting, dramatic, emergency-like response, as if I have the doctor on speed dial and he's waiting outside. The boys start laughing, I mix in a quick tickle, and I'm a miracle worker—the pain is gone! You're welcome.

Increase Personal Satisfaction

Laughter can also make it easier to cope with difficult situations. It also helps you connect with other people. Go figure! When was the last time you called up someone to go out with that you knew was a drag to be around? "Hey, I'm going to call Mark and see what he's up to tonight. I have no fun with him, and he never smiles"—said no one, ever, on planet Earth. I have teammates and friends all around North America. Who do you think I'm driving or flying to go see? The people who, I know, will be a blast to be around and will surely make me laugh. I also know that we built that bond over the years by laughing together. People want to be with people that make them smile. You want to be with people that make you smile, so be the person who laughs and smiles.

Consistency

*"How about you look at taking the rest of your life
to make it a part of your life."*
~ Jarrett Robertson

If you choose to start your New Year's resolution the week after January 1st, because that's when the holidays are officially over and things get back to "normal," you have already set yourself up for disappointment—the new year started on January 1st. Now, my intention is not to be the bearer of bad news but rather to give you a way that will guarantee your success.

Psychoanalysts say that only 8% of people follow through on their New Year's resolutions; and that, by far, the most popular New Year's resolution is to get in better shape, lose weight, get healthier, and live a better life. How about this? How about I give you an alternative goal that will allow you guaranteed success. It is quite literally the very first goal my coach and trainer gave to me: consistency.

Statistically, as mentioned above, only 8% of people follow through on their resolutions. I think that is because people try to make such a dramatic and life-altering change in such a short period of time. If health and fitness is your new goal in life, then how about you look at taking the rest of your life to make it a part of your life. My suggestion is to achieve consistency. I don't care if it is 20 minutes every Wednesday night after work, your goal is to NEVER miss a Wednesday. Perhaps it is 20 minutes once a week, but you NEVER miss that one time. If you start small with an idea or strategy like this, I PROMISE you will succeed. I don't care if you spend 2 years just doing 20 minutes every Wednesday night—guess what?—you're not part of the 92% who failed. After a while, when you are good and ready, add another 20-minute session, and spend however much time you need to make that a consistent part of your week/day. Consistency applies to all resolutions, not just fitness and health. The second most popular resolution is—you guessed it—to quit smoking. Try cutting down one cigarette a day or week, and do that until you are ready to cut out a second (or more); eventually, you will succeed. Even if you never completely quit, you have gone from a pack a day, down to just a couple. Guess what? Again, you're not part of the 92% who failed, because your goal was "CONSISTENCY."

Make it an amazing year!

Water

You do not need a physician, nutritionist, or even Dr. Oz to tell you that your body and system needs water. This is not groundbreaking news. You know, and you've always known it. The problem is that it is boring information and nothing "new."

Do you know that, as humans, we are the only mammals to drink milk from another animal? Plus, we are the only ones that drink it as a fluid source after nursing from the mother. In the wild, as soon as a calf, cub, fawn, colt, or even a puppy or kitten, are strong enough to be on their own and no longer need their mothers for food, they only drink water.

As a father, friend, colleague, leader, brother, son, husband, advisor, consultant, and business owner, my main objective is to educate: educate my clients, friends, and family on the WHY behind financial planning (i.e. insurance, investments, taxes, savings, spending, estates, etc.). For the most part, people get the WHAT and the HOW.

It's no different when it comes to your overall health and well-being. For the most part, you get the WHAT and the HOW: how to eat, what to eat, what not to eat, how to exercise, what exercises to do, what makes you feel good, how to feel good, what makes you feel bad, and so on.

I understand that when it comes to water and the sage advice of "drink it," I don't imagine anyone is falling off of their chair as they read this, thinking, "Jarrett changed my life!!"

However, just like I provide my clients a little more in-depth knowledge around the recommendations I am providing , perhaps these 4 reasons WHY drinking water is so vitally important to your overall health and well-being, will be just the catalyst you need to start drinking a little more H2O.

1) Drinking Water Helps Maintain the Balance of Bodily Fluids

The functions of these bodily fluids include digestion, absorption, circulation, creation of saliva, transportation of nutrients, and maintenance of body temperature. This is everything our bodies need to do in a day, and water helps them do it!! (Mic drop!)

2) Water Helps Energize Muscles

Cells that don't maintain their balance of fluids and electrolytes, shrivel, which can result in muscle fatigue. "When muscle cells don't have adequate fluids, they don't work as well, and performance can suffer," says Guest.

This goes for anyone and everyone. You don't have to be an athlete of any sort. We all have muscles; just some more than others. Regardless of who you are and how much muscle you have, you want them all to work and to work at their highest potential. On the days when you're hydrated properly, and everything is "ticking," guess what? You feel awesome.

3) Water Helps Your Kidneys

Body fluids transport waste products in and out of cells. "The main toxin in the body is blood urea nitrogen, a water-soluble waste that is able to pass through the kidneys to be excreted in the urine," explains Guest. "Your kidneys do an amazing job of cleansing and ridding your body of toxins as long as your intake of fluids is adequate." Toxins provide a myriad of health issues, both short and long-term. The quicker you can eliminate toxic waste in your body, the better off you'll be.

4) Water Helps Maintain Normal Bowel Function

Adequate hydration keeps things flowing along your gastrointestinal tract and prevents constipation. When you don't get enough fluid, the colon pulls water from stools to maintain hydration, and the result is constipation (no fun getting a workout while you're trying to get your poop out!).

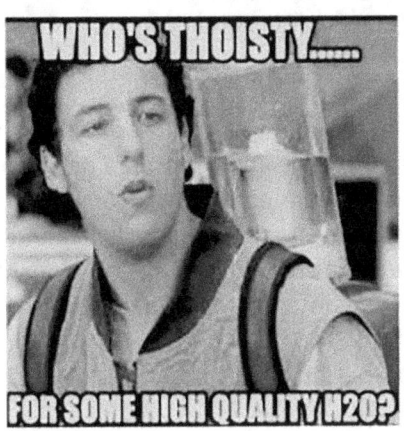

No Elevators and Park Far Away

Don't get me wrong; I'm not trekking up and down 30 flights of stairs on any given day. (My coach more than ensures I hit my recommended "floor" count in the vast majority of my programs, so I'm all good in that department.) Also, I'm not just trying to hit the daily recommended step count of 10,000.

Make It a Great Day

For me, the whole idea of parking a little further away, and taking the stairs instead of an escalator or elevator, is for the simple fact that I can. How many people in your life do you see, or people in general, that need the extra help, whether it is because of old age, an injury, or simple laziness? Trust me; one day that will be me (and it'll be you too). I will need help, I will need to park a little closer, and I'll 100% need to rely on elevators (for the record, I don't ever plan on being lazy); but today, I choose to walk those stairs and take an extra 15–30 seconds (literally) to park a little further away, because I can. How many times have you heard "don't take the little things for granted?" from someone who has been struck with a disability (short or long-term), an illness, or even worse, a tragedy? Listen, I'm not here to preach about how wonderful life is and that our world is made up of rainbows and butterflies; the purpose of this book is to give you a few small suggestions on the littlest things you can do that, in my opinion, will make you feel awesome.

My wife often gives me the "really?" look when we go out to do errands and end up at a Walmart or Home Depot, and I park where I do, passing 41 vacant spots on what people would label my "hike" to the store. It was 18 extra seconds; actually, I timed it. It's 18 seconds of fresh air, a few extra steps, more of a stretch, and perhaps just 18 extra seconds to hold onto my wife's hand or one of my kids.

Do the things you can do because you can!

> "The difference between what we do and
> what we are capable of doing
> would suffice to solve most of the world's problems.
> You must be the change you want to see in the world."
> ~ Gandhi

www.makeitagreatday.ca

Eat Cake in the Morning

Before you jump out of your chair and think I'm nuts, what I mean is to satisfy your cravings early in the day. Now, if you have a "craving" every single day, then you may want to tackle that issue prior to reading on. I see or hear of so many people who go about their day and, for dinner or a late night snack, they will indulge. I'm not saying I haven't done it, but what I am saying is that we can all probably agree that no good comes from it; and more importantly, you feel like absolute garbage (pretty much the polar opposite of what I'm trying to accomplish with this book). Satisfying your craving early in the day will do a few things for you:

It will do exactly that: satisfy your craving. Your body doesn't want pizza; your body doesn't want ice cream; your body doesn't want 2 lbs of wings; your body doesn't want a grilled cheese sandwich—your mind does. There is a little part of your brain that's responsible for cravings that won't go away until it's satisfied. It's just like a person poking you in the shoulder, or even worse, your kid saying, "Dad...Dad...Dad...Dad...Dad," until you say, "What!!? It's been 4 seconds, and I heard you the first time." Satisfy that craving early, and the "poking" goes away.

It actually gives you time to burn some of those calories. Your day will go on and, therefore, you will be burning calories. I'm not suggesting that you will burn off everything you took in, but what I am saying is that your net caloric intake at the end of the day will certainly be less than if you chose to indulge at the end of the day. You still have to walk around, get up and down from a chair, go to meetings, maybe think you're going to the gym; help with your children's activities; go for a walk and get some fresh air; or walk around the mall—all the things that you do in a day that burn calories—sitting; doing a mental exercise; working on project; responding to a phone call—that all burns calories, and it helps

You will make healthy choices the rest of the day (primarily because you have ticked off #1). Chances are that if you have 4 slices of pizza for lunch and then go on with your day, you're not pounding a burger and wings for dinner. You may make a better (and healthier) choice since earlier in the day, you know that you treated yourself.

You will still have a good night's rest (super important!). By the end of the day, you have satisfied your craving, managed to get through the rest of your day, and actually burned off some of those unwanted calories; so chances are, you will not, still, feel like garbage just before climbing into bed.

As I mentioned earlier, if you are fighting a "craving" every single day, then this particular part may not apply to you because, in reality, that is just your regular diet. For those of you (like me) who have that deep down craving every now and then, I'm suggesting to try and satisfy it early in the day. What do you have to lose? Remember, the whole point of this book is how to feel awesome. My goal, when the craving hits, is to make sure I feel good by the end of the day. The worst is feeling like garbage right before you go to sleep.

As Hard as You Can Go

If you have never heard or read about endorphins, you're missing out. We have all seen those infomercials on how to get fit in 3 minutes a day, or something ridiculous like that, and I'm not intending to challenge those theories (although you can well imagine what I think about them). When I say 20 minutes, I quite literally mean 20 minutes. From the time you sit on the bike, step up on the step mill, or sit down in the rower, 20 minutes later, you're all done. The catch here is "as hard as you can go"—and no, not for the entire 20 minutes; that's crazy!

High intensity interval training (HIIT) is a widely adopted method of training for high level athletes, extreme weight loss, and overall health and well-being. I'm not going to get into the science of HIIT, and I'm not here for a debate; this book is, once again, me sharing with you another way that you can feel awesome.

You're probably familiar with the term "runner's high," which refers to the euphoric feeling one sometimes gets when exercising. When your body crosses over from an aerobic state to an anaerobic state, it's suddenly operating without enough oxygen to satisfy the muscles and cells screaming out for it. This is when the "runner's high" occurs

I love it! Work your ass off and not only look incredible, which is why the vast majority of people work out, but also feel incredible because of the rush you'll get from your very own stash of feel-good drugs hidden deep inside your body and at your disposal. You just have to go and get them!

So, what are you waiting for!? Don't just hope for a great day; take control of your own mood, general well-being, and make it a great day. Crush yourself for 20 minutes (HIIT), and I promise you, you will feel awesome!

Chapter 2

Chemical Reaction

Tell Me More

Hormones are chemicals produced by different glands across your body. They travel through the bloodstream, acting as messengers and playing a part in many bodily processes.

One of these important functions? Helping regulate your mood. Certain hormones are known to help promote positive feelings, including happiness and pleasure. These "happy hormones" include: dopamine, serotonin, oxytocin, and endorphins.

Here are a few very small suggestions on how to improve your "happy hormones." You have always known about these activities—I call them the What and the How—but now you know the "Why," so that the next time you are taking a walk or petting your dog, know that you are actually improving your mental and physical well-being, and that's awesome!

Get Outside

Looking to boost your serotonin levels? Spending time outdoors, in sunlight, is a great way to do this. According to 2008 research, exposure to sunlight can increase production of both serotonin and endorphins.

Start with at least 10 to 15 minutes outside each day. It seems mundane, but I'm not the first one to tell you: Go for a walk. That's it, that's all. You may not feel it, and it may be boring, but know that you are increasing the serotonin in your system, and that is gold!

Maximize your workout to see even more benefits from exercise, including increased endorphins and serotonin levels:

Include a Few Friends

A small 2009 study looking at 12 men, found evidence to suggest that group exercise offers more benefits than solo exercise. I work hard when I train, and I'll go as far as to say that I definitely push myself far above the average person, but at no point since I stopped playing hockey and training with teammates, have I ever pushed myself so hard. The sheer benefit of having teammates, coaches, and trainers around will push you to your max, and the only person to benefit is you.

Laugh With a Friend

Who hasn't heard the old saying, "Laughter is the best medicine?"

Of course, laughter won't treat ongoing health issues. But it can help relieve feelings of anxiety or stress, and improve a low mood by boosting dopamine and endorphin levels.

According to a small 2017 study looking at 12 young men, social laughter triggered endorphin release.

So, share that funny video, dust off your joke book, or watch a comedy special with a friend or partner.

An added bonus? Bonding over something hilarious with a loved one, might even trigger oxytocin release. This is because you like being around people that make you laugh. Shocker!

Cook (and enjoy) a Favorite Meal With a Loved One

This tip could, in theory, boost all 4 of your happy hormones. To be honest, my wife and I, instead of ordering out once a weekend, signed up for a "farm to table" service that gets delivered once a week. All the ingredients, the recipe, and the instructions on exactly how to cook the entire meal are delivered to my door. My wife enjoys a glass of wine while I cook the selected meal (we get two per week), and we hang out and chat. I love cooking, and she loves having me cook for her, and it's a way for us to spend some time together.

The enjoyment you get from eating something delicious can trigger the release of dopamine, along with endorphins. Sharing the meal with someone you love, and bonding over meal preparation, can boost oxytocin levels.

Certain foods can also have an impact on hormone levels, so note the following when meal planning, for a happy hormone boost:

Spicy foods (which may trigger endorphin release), yogurt, beans, eggs, meats with a low-fat content, and almonds are just a few foods linked to dopamine release. Foods high in tryptophan have been linked to increased serotonin levels; and foods containing probiotics, such as yogurt, kimchi, and sauerkraut, can influence the release of hormones.

Listen to Music (or make some)

Music can give more than one of your happy hormones a boost.

Listening to instrumental music, especially music that gives you chills, can increase dopamine production in your brain.

But if you enjoy music, simply listening to any music you enjoy may help put you in a good mood. This positive change in your mood can increase serotonin production.

Musicians may also experience an endorphin release when creating music. According to 2012 research, creating and performing music, by dancing, singing, or drumming, led to endorphin release.

If you're familiar with meditation, you might already know of its many wellness benefits, from improving sleep to reducing stress. A small 2002 study links many of meditation's benefits to increased dopamine production during the practice. Research from 2011 also suggests that meditation can spur endorphin release.

Not sure how to start? It's not as hard as you might think. You don't even need to sit still, though it can help when you're first starting out.

If you are anything like me, the word "meditation" sounds hokey. Do you dream about things? Do you imagine being on a beach? Do you cry when thinking about happy times and past times? This is where it all started for me. Classical music in the car was extremely relaxing for me, and I found myself in a better state of mind. Happy thoughts came rushing in about my life, my family, my job, my dog, my kids, past teammates, weddings, trips, my workout, and the list goes on. It's not sitting with your legs crossed, humming your lips and doing your ohms, but if that works for you, then awesome!

Sit in a hot tub, a steam room, or a sauna, and just realize where you are. Take a drive and appreciate the scenery. I'll tell you, the best advice I can give you, to start any sort of self-awareness, is to talk about what you appreciate (in your head). It may seem strange, but if you tell your mind what to focus on and what to think, it will do exactly that. Your mind needs direction, and you need to tell it.

"I have healthy kids; they are awesome and they drive me crazy."

"I have a warm home and I'm so thankful for that. Man, my wife and I have worked hard for where we are at, and that's awesome."

"I have cable and can watch whatever I want."

"I have the best memories of teammates and past times."

"Cell phones and social media are the best, as they keep me connected to friends and family."

Whatever works for you is fine, as long as you just talk about the things in your life that are awesome.

Plan a Romantic Evening

Oxytocin's reputation as the "love hormone" is well-earned.

Simply being attracted to someone can lead to the production of oxytocin. But physical affection, including kissing, cuddling, or having sex, also contributes to oxytocin production.

Just spending time with someone you care about can also help boost oxytocin production. This can help increase closeness and positive relationship feelings, making you feel happy, blissful, or even euphoric.

If you really want to feel those happy hormones, note that dancing and sex both lead to endorphin release, while orgasm triggers dopamine release.

You can also share a glass of wine with your partner for an added endorphin boost.

Pet Your Dog

If you have a dog, giving your furry friend some affection is a great way to boost oxytocin levels, for you and your dog.

According to research from 2014, dog owners and their dogs see an increase in oxytocin when they cuddle.

Even if you don't own a dog, you might also experience an oxytocin boost when you see a dog you know and like. If you're a dog lover, this might happen when you get a chance to pet any dog at all.

So, find your favorite canine and give it a good ear scratch or lap cuddle.

One of my favorite analogies of all time is the definition of unconditional love. How do you actually define unconditional love?

If you lock your dog and your spouse in the trunk of your car and come back 6 hours later, who is excited to see you? Exactly! That's unconditional love. You're welcome.

Get a Good Night's Sleep

Not getting enough **quality** sleep can affect your health in multiple ways.

For one, it can contribute to an imbalance of hormones, particularly dopamine, in your body. This can have a negative impact on your mood as well as your physical health.

Setting aside 7 to 9 hours each night for sleep can help restore the balance of hormones in your body, which will likely help you feel better.

If you find it difficult to get a good night's sleep, try:

- Going to bed and getting up around the same time every day.
- Creating a quiet, restful sleeping environment (try reducing light, noise, and screens).
- Decreasing caffeine intake, especially in the afternoon and evening.
- Getting more tips on improving sleep.

Manage Stress

It's normal to experience some stress from time to time. But living with regular stress, or dealing with highly stressful life events, can cause drops in dopamine and serotonin production, and an increase in cortisol. This can negatively affect your health and mood, making it harder to deal with stress.

If you're under a lot of stress, the American Psychological Association recommends:

- Taking a brief break from the source of stress.
- Laughter.
- Taking 20 minutes for a walk, run, bike ride, or other physical activity.
- Meditation.
- Social interaction.

Any of these approaches may help relieve your stress while also boosting your levels of serotonin, dopamine, and even endorphins.

Get a Massage

If you enjoy massage, here's one more reason to get one: massage can boost all 4 of your happy hormones.

According to 2004 research, both serotonin and dopamine levels increased after massage. Massage is also known to boost endorphins and oxytocin.

You can get these benefits from a massage by a licensed massage therapist, but you can also get a massage from a partner for some extra oxytocin.

Let me tell you a story that will make all this make sense. I want you to envision athletes who, when they win a major championship game, or just have a huge victory of some sort, end up breaking down and crying. We call it "tears of joy." I've been there; I've won a few championships through my career, playing hockey, which I will never forget. I still have friends from those times. They were some of the best times of my life, and anyone who has ever won a championship of any kind, will tell you the same thing. Here's what's happening:

Throughout the game, throughout the week of practices, throughout the season, bucket loads of endorphins help mask the pain. They help you get through and to keep moving forward. You get endorphins when you're working that hard, and it's awesome. Picture an athlete scoring a goal, scoring a touchdown, getting a base hit or homerun, hitting a basket, driving across the line, running to the finish line, and so on. Any athlete in any sport has a goal in mind. Every small step along the way gives them a hit of dopamine. It's a small reward so that you'll keep coming back. It's a small reward so that you'll continue to pursue the ultimate goal. Dopamine will help you come back when you don't score the goal, get stopped, get struck out, or don't get to the end zone. You got there before, and dopamine allows you to keep coming back. It gives you the reason to continue the chase. Next, you get a surge of serotonin from the crowd that screams your name, from your teammates that celebrate you—you get a surge of serotonin because you're so proud and happy that you've worked so hard and you've achieved this goal. Endorphins, dopamine, and serotonin—all these feelings come to fruition.

Then there's that final championship game or winning moment when the buildup is finally over. You often hear people say, "the blood, sweat, and tears," which are the visual attributes of dopamine, endorphins, and serotonin. The game is over, the championship is won, and the teammates embrace each other, and you see tears. There is an avalanche of oxytocin—the love chemical, the greatest chemical of all—the chemical that brings us together as humans and bonds us. The connection is so powerful, and that's where you see the tears. These chemicals are so paramount for us in society. You just see it more dramatically in sporting events. It's mind boggling to watch "behind the scenes" of what it takes for people to prepare. Whether it is a sport, a business, or is personal—you name it—the prep that goes into achieving success is riddled with these chemicals. If you understand what they are, how to get them, what they do for you, and why they are so important, once again, I promise you will feel awesome.

Dopamine

Also known as the "feel-good" hormone, dopamine is a hormone and neurotransmitter that's an important part of your brain's reward system. Dopamine is associated with pleasurable sensations, along with learning, memory, motor system function, and more.

If "Ping! Buzz! or Ring!" are any part of your day, you get hammered with dopamine all day long. "Likes" on social media, notifications, emails, and text are scientifically designed to hook you in. In fact, Dr. Nir Eyal created a theory called "Hooked," to prove exactly what is happening to you, and explains what social media has done.

Dopamine is highly addictive and can be a major problem if you do not control it. There are age limits and restrictions on things like alcohol and gambling, but no age restrictions on dopamine-producing events.

Make It a Great Day

Have you ever heard of someone who removed themselves from social media because they wanted to "take a break?" What about those friends who decide to go "dry" for a month because they want to give their body a break from booze? See the resemblance? When I learned more about this, the first step I took was turning off every notification and sound on my phone, for anything and everything. The reason is that I understand I was being controlled by the dopamine hits every single time my phone or email went off. Now I control when I look at my phone for texts or emails, and I decide when to look at social media. Don't believe me? Leave your phone on, and the next time you are having an important conversation or are in a meeting, and a ping or buzz comes through, I want you to see if you can truly concentrate and not worry about the email or text that is sitting on your phone. I promise you that the hit of dopamine in your system will shift your mind right to your phone.

The amazing part about dopamine is that it is designed to make sure we move forward and get things done. A check list, even if you're not a "to-do" list type of person, actually gives you tiny hits of dopamine every time you cross off something you completed: "Yes, check, done!" Mile markers for marathon runners are an absolute necessity, or they would never complete the race. Tiny hits of dopamine hit your system every time you get to the next marker, which boosts you to keep going. Quarterly targets, albeit arbitrary, give employees, shareholders, leaders, and companies a target so that they can work to achieve a goal. Dopamine is so paramount in our days, both good and bad. If you learn the benefits of dopamine and where it occurs in your life, you can take the steps to make sure it helps you. For me, it's turning off all sounds (trust me, you won't miss anything; try it) and checking things off with enthusiasm. Boom! Done!

Endorphins

The reason I continue to lead an active life is not solely for my physical appearance. I do it because it makes me feel good, helps me be less stressed, and prevents diseases, and just because I like it. The body's natural feel-good chemicals, released during exercise, are called endorphins. Endorphins are your body's natural pain reliever, which your body produces in response to stress or discomfort. Endorphin levels also tend to increase when you engage in reward-producing activities, such as eating, working out, or having sex.

Ah, the natural, feel-good drug! When you exercise, endorphins are released to produce feelings of euphoria and general well-being. What else is super cool about endorphins is that they act as a natural painkiller. I think about the days when I am dragging my ass to the gym because I am so tired from work or whatever else. After 15–20 minutes of warming up, and then a few sets of an exercise, all of a sudden, I'm smiling, my eyes are wide open, I've got energy, and I'm just all around in a better mood. Why's that? Because I am high on endorphins, aka awesomeness.

Interesting fact: Researchers have found that light to moderate weight training or cardiovascular exercise doesn't produce endorphins; only heavy weights or training that incorporates sprinting or other anaerobic exertion does this.

Serotonin

This hormone (and neurotransmitter) helps regulate your mood as well as your sleep, appetite, digestion, learning ability, and memory.

Research shows that an estimated 90% of the body's serotonin is produced in the gut, where it influences gut immunity. I learned this a few years ago and set out to ensure that my gut health was as optimal as I could make it. It's not an overnight process as there is a ton to learn. The reason why I encourage you to learn about gut health is for the benefits of serotonin. Something I say to friends, family, and even clients, as an analogy, is that if there was a machine that printed money, and it sat in your basement—let's say that machine printed $100 bills—would you not do everything in your power every day to protect that machine? You would make sure the power never went out, no one ever got close to it, and that it was bubble wrapped, water resistant, and bulletproof, and that it had all the battery power or electricity it would ever need—you name it. You would never want that machine to break, and you would want it to be optimal all the time. Think of your gut as the machine that prints money, only that the monetary value in this case is serotonin. I encourage you to improve your gut health in order to be able to maximize the serotonin that you can tap into on a daily basis.

Oxytocin

Often called the "love hormone," oxytocin is essential for childbirth, breastfeeding, and strong parent-child bonding. This hormone can also help promote trust, empathy, and bonding in relationships, and oxytocin levels generally increase with physical affection like kissing, cuddling, and sex.

This chemical is all the rainbows and butterflies, my favorite chemical of all. How is it that a mother can sit with their child for 3 hours on the couch, without moving, so that their child can sleep? What the hell am I tearing up for when my kid took his first stride on the hockey rink? What is happening when you hug your spouse or best friend with sincere appreciation? You are getting this flood of oxy- tocin, and it's awesome.

I have a bond with a few buddies that dates back over 30 years in a few of the cases, and the things we have been through are a book on its own. Like many of you reading this book, I hope you have relationships out there that are unexplainable. What I'm telling you is that there is a proven reason you are so close, trust them with everything, and would do anything for them. Oxytocin has been filling you up over the years and has formed a bond that is unbreakable. I learned this, I know this, and I now thrive on it. I call these people all the time just to talk about anything and everything, and I make a point to go and see them because I want to, and I know it's healthy for both of us. I continue to search for more oxytocin because it's healthy and so awesome.

Here is a really cool thing about oxytocin. Simple acts of human generosity increase your oxytocin. Just helping someone, out of the goodness of your heart, will give you a boost of oxytocin. The catch is that it has to be genuine. I was at Costco loading a bbq into the trunk of my car, and out of nowhere, the gentleman next to me simply came over and said, "Hey, let me help you with that." I didn't ask; and to be honest, I didn't need the help, but it was fabulous and I truly appreciated it. Oxytocin not only flooded my system but it flooded his as well. Here is the best part: Just witnessing an act of human generosity increases your oxytocin. His wife, who was standing watching, and any other person in the parking lot, would have gotten an increase in oxytocin just by witnessing his help. Research shows that the more oxytocin you have in your body, the more generous and willing to help you are. There is a significant chance that the people who witnessed the act of generosity, if given the chance later that day or week, in turn, helped someone else as well. Oxytocin is known to inhibit addiction, increase your immune system, help you to be better at solving problems, and increase your creativity.

Cortisol

Cortisol is the other chemical that is responsible for so many things. While writing this book, I learned that cortisol has a half-life of 18 minutes. Why I say that is because the other thing that cortisol will do is limit our ability to communicate and think effectively. When you are highly anxious or feeling stressed, there is a surge of cortisol in your brain that starts to shut down various parts and puts you into protection mode. Think of the last time you had an argument with a colleague, spouse, child, or friend, and you all of a sudden "couldn't think straight." Guess what? You're right! Cortisol had taken your brain hostage. Fast forward 30 minutes, a few hours, or a couple of days, and what do you say to yourself? "I should have said that," or "I should have said this." The problem is that in the moment, you did not have the capability.

Cortisol comprises your immune system and inhibits the release of oxytocin. Biologically, if you feel unsafe in an environment, you are less empathetic and less generous. You care less about the people around you because cortisol is telling you to care about yourself. It is protecting you. You can't have energy to help other people when you are too busy protecting yourself. Something has to give.

Think of cortisol as nature's built-in alarm system. It's your body's main stress hormone. It works with certain parts of your brain to control your mood, motivation, and fear.

It temporarily shuts down the body's systems in the face of crisis such as digestion and reproduction.

My coach, through my days of competing in the fitness industry, as we got closer to the competition day, would often check in to make sure I wasn't freaking out (i.e. stressed out) because we were not where we were supposed to be, and our results wouldn't be optimal. I came to learn that he never really actually cared about me; he knew that by stressing out or worrying, my cortisol levels would increase, effectively shutting down important functions (i.e. digestion), and as he so politely put it, "You'll be fat." All kidding aside, this guy cared a ton, not only for me but for all of his athletes. This is the first experience I had with cortisol.

Cortisol is meant to be in and out of your body. The moment you know that cortisol is present, the moment you can take steps to get rid of it. As I mentioned earlier, cortisol has an 18-minute half-life. So, what do you do? Take a walk; get some fresh air. In fact, oxygen is known to be a catalyst in helping oxidize cortisol. Revisit the situation at a later date; sleep on it. If cortisol limits your ability to think and communicate effectively, is it in your best interest and the other parties' best interests to come back?

Chapter 3

In a Day

News

The news once was tasked with providing you information on events that were happening around the world or around your area, but I suppose it depended on which news channel you tuned into. Nowadays, the news is mandated to provide you information that in turn will drive up their ratings in order to increase their bottom line. When, at any point in time, was it beneficial for me to know that two cars collided in a city 200 kilometres away, and that someone was in critical condition? Listen, if it was my family member, relative, colleague, or friend, I wouldn't need any news media outlet to let me know what's happening. I would find out.

I have purposely not watched the news in over 5 years, and I promise you that I know everything that I need to know. How? Because everyone else on planet Earth, and on social media, will tell you their thoughts, feelings, and opinions. If something catches my attention, or someone informs me about something, guess what? I can go and watch it or find out more about it, at anytime, anywhere.

Our brains are only 2%–3% of our entire body weight, but they use 25% of our caloric intake. That is a highly inefficient machine and, therefore, is ALWAYS looking for ways to conserve energy. No machine can function at that capacity. The average human is tasked with making 12.7M decisions a year; that's 30+ thousand per day. It is impossible for every decision to be carefully thought out; it's straining, and it can't happen. Therefore, we go with what is familiar in order to conserve energy for the times we have to think.

Research proved that when people who watch financial news were hooked up to an FMRI, the part of the brain responsible for critical thinking and decision making went to sleep. The brain chooses to believe what it is hearing because it's from "experts," and it saves energy to not have to think.

Let's look at any announcement, anywhere, at any time. Political announcements, sports, finance, whatever interests you have, you have the ability to find out about this on your own time. I had a very interesting conversation with a family member about watching the news, and their response was that they needed to watch the news, not once but TWICE a day, in order to know what is going on in the world. To their benefit, they are from the baby boomer generation, where they grew up on the local news—I get it. It's how you found out about stuff. Plus, their parents had radios on, with the news, their whole lives as well. It's seared into their daily regime.

Here is what I have learned: By starting off the day with information that is given to you, without the choice to decide whether or not you want to hear it, completely 100% unequivocally affects your day. I'm fascinated by people who believe they can just listen to the news and that it has no effect on their day's events.

The roads are bad; there have been multiple accidents; avoid driving if you can. Well, we're not going to Grandma and Grandpa's today so that we can go sledding and play outside; the roads are bad. Wait a minute; what about the several thousand vehicles that made it safe and sound to their destinations? How about deploying news that tells me how people are moving much slower today and are being very cautious so that they can get to Grandma and Grandpa's and have an amazing day outside with family and friends.

I'm not suggesting that we turn our heads and be naïve or ignorant; that's the last thing I would ever do. What I know is that there are things I love, and things that make me feel amazing, so I choose to watch, listen, read, research, and do those things. Continuing with the above example and the twice-a-day news watcher, I asked what it was that they enjoyed doing in a day, and further to that, what was most important to them. They replied, "Family, the outdoors, walking, traveling, and grandkids." From there, I then simply suggested to why not watch things about the outdoors, or where the best places are to walk or travel, or how to become a better grandparent, or maybe look at pictures of her family—anything that you control, that you could watch, learn, or research, that has to do about the things you love and you love to do. Maybe listen to music that you love hearing, as opposed to turning on the news and listening about an accident, murder, bad news about finances, or that you can't travel to these parts of the world because of X, Y, and Z. Your mood is immediately affected by what you've heard, what you've listened to, and what you have seen. You don't control that you've taken in this information from an external source, and now you have to decide how to deal with it.

If you just listened to some news that was not positive, and you went out to see some friends, I can almost certainly guarantee that the first thing you talk about is, "Oh, did you hear about... or did you see ...?" And thus, you start your day off by talking about bad news with your friends, when really you should be there saying, "How are you?" "What's going on?" Look how sunny it is today." "It's really nice that we get to connect and have a coffee and just be with each other." How much better is that as opposed to "the weather sucks," or "This is what happened," or "I can't believe what's going on over there," and "Did you hear about this or did you hear about that?" The news, for me, once I learned how it affected my day and how I was feeling, has simply become a resource of negative information. Sure, there are positive stories, absolutely, but if all the news did was give you good news every day—"Hey, my kid did really well in gym," "Hey, my kid got their driver's license today," "Hey, there were 381 thousand vehicles that made it safe to work today," "Did you know that two friends went for coffee and had a great chat?"—it just wouldn't sell, and people would stop watching it. I control my day; I control what I listen to, watch, and hear, and that in turn helps me make it a great day. You can't un-hear or un-see something, so be extremely selfish and picky on what you let in.

If you start your day off watching the news or social media, and you're wondering how you can change that, you'll find something in the next chapter that is really cool, which I learned over the years and has been an enormous help in my day-to-day. More importantly, I'll tell you the effects it had on me.

Schedule

Ever have those days where it feels like everything is coming at you all at once and you can't catch up? Let me answer that for you: Yes! What about those days that are smooth sailing? What if there was a way for you to be able to be on the smooth sailing boat, each and every day? Here is the deal: No matter what you read from here, moving forward in this section, rest assured there are still going to be days that get away from you and are chaotic. I apologize for being the bearer of that news, but that's just reality.

I learned a technique through a leadership program I registered for, and it has, for all intents and purposes, fundamentally changed how I attack my day. I can say this with confidence because, on the days that I do not implement this strategy, more often than not, it is not a "great" day.

We all have the same amount of time in a day, days in a week, weeks in a month, and months in a year. Further to that, you are only human and can only accomplish so much in a day. It's just common sense that you cannot do it all.

What I learned, and what I want to pass along to you, is to take the time, the night before, to write down your schedule for the next day. The concept that was introduced to me was being the CEO and employee. Things have to get done whether it is at work or at home, so to end your evening, as the CEO, you write down everything you need your "employee" to accomplish the next day. In any place of employment, the boss lays out their expectations and hires the people they feel will accomplish the job. As the employee, you don't ask questions, and you get the work done. I think you see where I am going here, but let's go a step further.

As the CEO, you write down everything that needs to get accomplished the following day, without any regard for what the employee thinks. You are the CEO in this moment, and these things need to be completed. The next morning, when you wake up as the employee, you have your schedule and task for the day, and you simply do what you are told.

In my experience, what I have found is that on the days I truly do write out what I am doing, literally every hour, I am so much more relaxed, I get much more accomplished, I remain focused, and best of all, my stress levels are nil. The challenge I had when I first started this exercise was that I actually enjoyed some spontaneity in my day, and did not love the idea of having my entire day structured. So, what did I do? I scheduled in, "11 a.m. to 12 p.m.: Whatever comes up"; or 3 p.m. to 4 p.m.: Do what you want," and it helped. There is no right or wrong way to success with this idea; there is just your way and what works for you.

What is so important to take away from here is that by scheduling your day, you control your mood, anxiety, stress, cortisol, digestion, focus, and motivation. You see, fear and uncertainty are things that will immediately inhibit our ability to have a great day. Our bodies and minds will go into survival mode and work to protect us in whatever way they can. It's how we are built as human beings. The 2-million-year-old computer, inside of our heads, is built to take care of us, so in the face of fear and uncertainty, we will biologically default to taking care of #1, ourselves.

When I first started this activity, like I said, I was a little hesitant, and it took me some time to figure it out. Once I found a rhythm, it dawned on me that this had nothing to do with the fact that the CEO in me was getting more out of the employee; but rather, as the employee, my days were so much better. I was a better husband, a better father, a better colleague, and a better leader; I had better workouts, and I made better decisions when it came to eating, and the list goes on. By figuring out a schedule and the things that needed to get done the next day, or even just things that I wanted to do (if it was a weekend with my kids), I had control, and I made it a great day!

Social Media

Social media came into my life, I think, around 1996, with ICQ. I remember Myspace, and I remember when Facebook was first introduced in 2004, because I actually was at school at the time, and Facebook was released to the Ivy League universities. Without knowing at the time what social media was for, as it was being launched again, everyone was connecting with one another. It was fun and it was a way to connect with old friends from high school, from back home, as I was traveling all the time, and it was amazing. Fast forward 20 years, social media has been amazing, and it has also been detrimental for so many people and so many companies. I've chosen to use social media for marketing purposes to get my name out there because I've always said to any of my staff, colleagues ,advisors, friends, and family, that if you're not on the Internet nowadays, you don't exist; or if you're not on social media, you don't exist. I'm sure some people would argue that, and it's unfair to say.

I certainly agree that there's a lot of different ways to build your brand and get your name out there. But I don't think many people would argue that the minute someone recommends, refers, or suggests a name of a person, company, vacation destination, or resort, the first thing people do, within let's say 30 seconds, is to check on Google. What can I find out about that company, person, place, or thing that other people are saying things about? Heck, companies have grown, and companies have been created just to bring people together who are talking about people, places, and things—companies like TripAdvisor and Yelp. Here are my thoughts on social media: If you don't have the emotional capacity to be able to go on social media and recognize that this is a moment in time for this person, place, or thing that you're looking at, then try your best to avoid it. Don't get me wrong; I like social media, and I go on it and I check things out, but nothing on social media paints the entire picture. It's impossible. The only way social media could be real is if I took a video or took a picture of every moment of my day: all the private situations; all the public situations; all the conversations with my staff, my children, and my wife; all the good times and the bad times; and the times when I wake up in the morning, and how terrible I look; and then, all of a sudden, how amazing I look when I'm all dressed up. Where I think social media has a detrimental effect on someone's day is the comparison: "Am I as good as that person? Why am I not on a beach when I work so much harder and so much longer? I can't afford that; how do they drive that car? Look how happy their relationship is, and their kids are angels 24/7." Come on! You don't know the whole story, and you don't know the whole picture, yet all you tell yourself and convince yourself is that you might not be as good, or that you need to be better. That will absolutely have an effect on your day.

When I go on social media, I choose to go on there for entertainment purposes. "That person looks great. Look at them on a beach; they are working out—super! The kids looks awesome; they seem to be happy. Mmm, their steak looks well-cooked and delicious." I don't know the back story, and I have no idea where they came from, but I know lots of people who look fantastic but are depressed. I know lots of people who drive the nicest cars but are dead broke, and I know people who are traveling but are alone. Without having the entire picture, it's really hard on your psyche to be on social media. Ten different takes, fifteen different filters—you're presenting yourself to the world, or you're presenting your business, place, or thing to the world, which is seen through the eyes of these filters. That's one thing I've learned when I go on social media. And that's one thing that I promised myself—when I go on and I start to look at Facebook, Instagram, LinkedIn, and the plethora of other platforms—that I quite frankly won't use. I'm very aware of filters and what they do.

One of my best friends has a story that would blow anyone off their chair, and his Instagram page is rainbows and butterflies, which I love seeing. And I love going on there because I know where he came from, and it almost brings a tear to my eye every time I see these pictures, but I know that whole story. What people wouldn't know when going on there, is his entire background. I'm learning more and more today from listening to my nieces and nephews, who are getting into the preteen years, about the absolute carnage it is having on their emotional intelligence, on their social skills, and on their friendships. It is wild to watch; if they don't get a certain number of likes, or if someone in particular doesn't comment, they go into a downward spiral. They will change everything they do because that's what we've done in society. We've conditioned someone that if you're not liked on social media, then you're not valued.

There is an incredible video that I want you to watch. It's called "Hooked," by Dr. Nir Eyal. He talks about the science behind what makes technology so habit forming. This will fundamentally change your view and approach to online shopping, browsing, YouTube, and social media. This video and proof has allowed me to realize what's happening in the moment, so that I can, effectively, break out of it. It's the reason why you are glued to your phone and the reason why it chemically controls you.

Sleep

On average, it's an agreed upon metric that you should get 8 hours of sleep per night. Some can sleep less, and by that, I mean 7 or 7.5 hours, and some may need a little more. Working with 8 hours on average, then that works out to be 33% of your day. Let's think about this: 33 % of your day, week, month, and year are spent sleeping. How much thought, time, resources, and money do you put into the setup of your room, the type of mattress you have, the kind of pillows you use, your blankets, the temperature of your room, the humidity levels, and the ambience? If you are like the vast majority of society, and anything like I was before learning more, you put in very little time and very little thought.

How is it that people will go to great lengths to purchase custom orthotics or custom shoes, research and build custom cars that display who they are, get custom clothes/suits made, and even custom hats, yet they give little to no thought to customizing a place in which they spend 1/3 of their lives.

I learned a lot from Dr. Matt Walker, through various TED Talks and Audible books on the Science of Sleep. The single most important thing I learned was that each and every one of us has what's called a circadian rhythm. A circadian rhythm is a natural, internal process that regulates the sleep-wake cycle and repeats on each rotation of the Earth, roughly every 24 hours. It can refer to any biological process that displays an endogenous, entrainable oscillation of about 24 hours.

I recommend following Dr. Walker to get some eye-opening information on what exactly is happening when you sleep. Once you learn about your circadian rhythm, it will be an "aha" moment for you, and your habits will change; I promise. Seeing that you have to sleep every single night of your life (perhaps you skipped a few in your lifetime, but you know how that feels), sleeping is the second longest thing you'll ever commit to in your life. The first is being awake. People just do not or have not taken the time to learn how important it is.

I want to win at sleeping. I know that sounds odd, but it's the only way I know how to pass the message on to you. I want to be the best I can be at sleeping every night. And guess what? Sometimes I'm terrible at it, and sometimes I outright lose, but that's okay. It's 1/3 of my life; I'm not going to get it right every time. My goal is to wake up the next morning and say, "WHOA!! Nailed it; let's go!"

The greatest athletes in the world do not eat an abundance of unhealthy food, or food that will make them feel terrible right before playing a game. You don't get drunk before you work, play a big game, or before a big meeting. Why not? These are activities that have a finite time in your life. Work will end, the game will end, and the meeting will be over, yet people want to win and will do everything they can to be their best in those situations. Don't get me wrong; I do as well. However, it was not until I learned more about sleeping and the domino effect it had, where I was able to have more control and be consistently better in those situations. By treating sleep as the single biggest championship game you have ever played in, or the single biggest meeting you'll ever be a part of, you set yourself up to be the best version of you from the moment you wake up. You will be better at making decisions; you will have higher tolerance for your children, colleagues, spouse, society, employees, politics, and government. You will control stress better, you will crush your workouts, and you will be more focused and far more motivated.

I'm not reinventing the wheel by telling you to not scroll through your phone while you lie in bed, or watch the news right before you go to sleep. If you are, my first suggestion is to just give it a try. I do not check any social media, or open emails or texts, or watch any news as I'm getting ready to hit the hay. Remember that any information you take in from an external source is automatically downloaded by the amygdala and assigned an emotion. I simply have no desire to see, read, or hear something that could affect my ability to be the best I can be before going to sleep. Of course, I could see something that makes me extremely happy; I've absolutely thought of that, but that's a chance. I'm happy to scroll through pictures on my own, of times with my friends, moments with my kids, and memories of trips with my wife—absolutely.

Simon Sinek talks about vision in corporations because we need to see something in order to work toward it; we need to see our goal, and that's why it is called a vision—we can see it. You can watch athletes, before any game, do visualizing. Watch a basketball player on a free throw line before a game winning shot—what are they doing? They'll close their eyes and see the ball going through the hoop. When the famous Babe Ruth was calling his shot, guess what? He wasn't visualizing striking out.

If I want to have the best sleep, I want to make sure my mind is in the right place, and this means that I control what goes in prior to falling asleep. This does not mean that I visualize sleeping (that's boring), but it does mean that I ensure my entire environment is set up to give me the best chance at being awesome at sleeping. My entire day depends on my quality of sleep. It has nothing to do with quantity, and everything to do with quality.

Work

Are You Letting Your Emotions Run Your Meetings?

One of the secrets to running effective meetings that most people don't realize is emotion management.

When strong emotions are stirred up during a meeting, they can completely derail the meeting and steer it away from its goals. Defensiveness and anger have no place in a business meeting. They can only damage it, and they never produce good results.

Since the meeting room isn't the place for outbursts and meltdowns, strong emotions have to be managed well.

Prepare Thoroughly

There is less chance for emotional explosions in a meeting that's tightly structured. Prepare the meeting well and create a detailed schedule. Try to anticipate which areas may be emotional, and create a contingency plan for dealing with them if trouble arises.

Employ Empathy

When strong emotions erupt, try to handle it calmly. Start by putting yourself in the other person's shoes. What are they feeling that is causing the outburst? Rather than condemning them for letting their emotions get the best of them, try to see the situation through their eyes. Remember that they are "right" in their mind.

If you can see it through the other person's eyes, you'll better understand how to defuse the situation. You can also let them know that you understand, and this can also calm them down.

Take a Break

A great strategy for dealing with strong emotions during meetings is to simply take a break and cool down. This is the business meeting version of counting down from ten and taking deep breaths.

Leave the meeting room and let everyone go their separate way so that they can decompress. Give it five or ten minutes, or however much time you deem necessary for everyone to cool down and process their emotions. Come back to the meeting when everyone is feeling more calm and collected.

Apologize Quickly and Easily

It's very easy for people who are emotionally intelligent to say that they're sorry. These simple words can defuse many tense situations. An apology may be all the upset person wants to hear.

The outburst may not be your fault, but learn to apologize easily. Apologizing shows sympathy, and it shows that you understand how the other person feels.

No Blame

Things get heated quickly when there are accusations and blame. Try never to blame someone in a meeting, even if they clearly did something wrong. This is almost sure to trigger defensiveness and all of the strong emotions that come with it. Instead, identify a problem that exists for the meeting to solve.

Know Your Own Emotions

Get to know your own emotions and emotional triggers. Even if a meeting gets out of hand, keep yourself calm and learn to deal with your emotions appropriately. Develop your own emotional intelligence and let it help you keep things under control.

Phone a Friend

In my back pocket, I have a list of people that I can call. This was something I learned in a program I took with Randy Taylor, called Taylormade Leadership. This became an outlet if I was having a rough time, moment, or day. Even if I wasn't having a rough moment or anything like that, I would just pick up the phone and call, because these people made me happy and maybe even laugh, or just took my mind from the place I was in; I got to be silly, reminisce about old times, talk about past times, or anything. My best friend and I, who I've known for 33 years, talk arguably every day or every couple of days, and the phone call could last 90 seconds to an hour. I'm not even sure what we talk about half the time, and I don't think he does either. We check in to see what's going on, and half the time, it's nothing—he could be stopping to get a coffee, heading into work, or picking up his daughters. He'll put me on hold, I'll hang up, call him later, or whatever happens. It's just hearing each other's voices; that's it: a small little tap to say I'm here and that I always will be.

I have other buddies I'll check in on as well, to see what's going on, get an update, and hear about what they're doing and how work is going—we just shoot the shit. I have one particular buddy that I call, and I swear if anyone heard our conversation, they would be spinning around in circles, wondering if it was even English. One of my roommates from college, and I, have basically created our own language, and all we do is hysterically laugh for about 9 to 15 minutes. We've built that relationship and bond, and that's the best part of all. We will call each other randomly, and it's an automatic good time. My sister and I talk, probably once a week or once every couple of weeks. It could be in depth, could be for nothing, could be just be to catch up, or could be for her to be able to talk to my kids, or for many other reasons. I know that a lot of people would say, "Well, she's family," but she has always been more than that; she's a friend. I'll call her on my drives just to hear her voice as well, for no good reason. It's comforting; we laugh, we sing songs, we talk about old times—all that stuff. I'm big on connecting with people that are fun to speak with: people that I know will make me laugh; people that I know I can make laugh, or perhaps help them in their day and inspire them—whatever it is. The point of this is that I've made a conscious effort, and a list, to pick up the phone and call the people I know I'm closest with, to maintain that relationship. At the end of the day (and definitely when I get off the phone), I feel fantastic and my day is better.

Chapter 4

Take Control

Amygdala Hijacking

Have you ever lashed out at your kid, spouse, colleague, or friend because of something they did or said that made you angry, frustrated, or annoyed, and you immediately realized that there may have been a better approach? Have you ever tried a food and immediately said out loud, while you spit it out, "Eww … gross?"

Have you ever (silently) judged someone simply by looking at them? Yes, you have!!

When we feel, touch, taste, see, or hear, that information is immediately directed to an area of the brain called the amygdala: the part of the brain responsible for emotions. This is an uncontrollable event. The point of this is that our brains are always in survival mode and must assign an emotion prior to making any decisions. From here, the information makes its way to the rational and irrational part of the brain, where a decision is made. This is controllable. "Amygdala hijack" was coined by Daniel Goleman, and it refers to a "personal, emotional response that is immediate, overwhelming, and out of measure with the actual stimulus, because it has triggered a much more significant emotional threat." There are some very hot and significant events happening right now in all of our lives, and every single one of us will respond differently. One of the most relevant is our current working environment. There are days that I am annoyed, frustrated, and demotivated, and others where I'm happy, thankful, and checking off everything on my "to-do" list. What I know is that the emotional response is from an external source (i.e. info I take in), but how I choose to react (i.e. decision) is internal.

It is 100% in your control as to what information you allow your brain to receive. Just be aware that it will trigger some kind of emotional response before a decision can be made. If you want to be happy, I suggest watching or listening to something, eating, or doing an activity that you know will make you happy. Are some days more challenging than others? Absolutely; but you still have that control. Even when I'm with my 5 and 3-year-old, it feels like I am 100% not in control—they are driving me bananas, and simply the sound of the word "Dad" sends shivers down my spine—but I do control how I respond.

One of my primary jobs as an advisor is to equip our clients with the tools and knowledge that will help set them up for success (financially).

There's no difference in providing yourself with the tools and knowledge, mentally and emotionally, so that you can be the best *you*! Whether that is to be the best advisor, spouse, leader, colleague, friend, sibling, son/daughter, parent, or business owner, if you do not have the tools, how can you win?

If you have made it this far in the book, how many comments and thoughts have you had to this point (because there were a lot)? What will you do from here?

The choice is yours!

Fear

This is a topic/emotion that so many people are dealing with right now, and in so many different ways. It relates to both our personal and professional lives. Did you know that babies (which include you) are only born with two fears—the fear of falling and the fear of loud noises? Over the course of your life, every other "fear" has been learned or accepted by an external source. Parents, friends, and colleagues were the main source for many years, and in today's society, that external source is primarily from the news and social media.

In the wake of 9/11, 1600 people died due to automobile fatalities because they were too scared to fly. It is the safest form of travel in the world. In 2018, 50 times as many people died from taking selfies than from shark attacks, and yet we are all scared of sharks.

Don't get me wrong; I get angry and I experience fear, but I don't stay there. (Mentally) I get the hell out of there as quick as possible, and for good reason.

Whether you follow, like/dislike, or have even heard of Tony Robbins, he's not reinventing the wheel.

https://youtu.be/vGfTrW328JI

Fear

It is a hormonal response (uncontrollable). Your heart starts to race, you start to breathe shallowly, and everything narrows down your focus.

We go into survival mode because we have a 2-million-year-old brain that always looks for what's wrong so that it can protect us from it. The unfortunate part is that so many people tap into that, and it dictates their day (controllable).

If you are in a fearful state or angry state, you see everything differently (controllable). You see everything through those filters (that's because our brains are in "survival" mode).

When you are grateful, it DESTROYS the two emotions that mess us up: fear and anger. You cannot be grateful and fearful at the same time. You cannot be grateful and angry at the same time. When people are uncertain (i.e. fearful), they do not take action.

Athletes envision making the shot, scoring the goal, hitting the home run, and winning the race for a reason. It puts them in a state of mind to continuously practice and never give up. It's a trained mind!

In business, imagining the "big" sale and how that plays out—maybe having your own dream office space, qualifying for a conference and being amongst the top, and building an elite team—or whatever your professional goals are, if you are scared or fear that none of this will ever happen, then you're probably right.

Thank you for what you do. You fundamentally help improve the lives of so many people. That's awesome!

Music

Most of us have learned that music is for entertaining. Let's be honest; no one is traveling on a plane to tailgate and then file into a stadium full of fans to listen to spa music. Music, as it turns out, encourages creativity and helps us become more productive. I never really trusted this until I took a moment to stop (listen) and recognize the music I was listening to, on the days when I seemed to get the absolute most accomplished.

I'm not sure why, but I started listening to classical music around the age of 35. As a matter of fact, as I write this section of the book, I am sitting in my office on a Sunday morning, listening to a playlist on

Spotify, called Morning Classical. I found that I was turning to classical music on my drive home later at night from work or a meeting, and also after I would train at night. It was an immediate means of relaxing and telling myself that it was time to calm down. I then started reflecting on where and when I would hear classical music: spas (that one is easy), some lounges and bars, libraries, coffee shops, museums, resting areas, and perhaps different rooms while you wait for an appointment. The point is this: Listening to music can also be therapeutic, relieving feelings of stress so that you can concentrate better. Research suggests that there are 6 kinds of music to listen to that can help you improve your mood, relieve stress, concentrate better, be more productive, increase your focus, and feel awesome. Note that 4 out of 6 recommendations (and potentially 6/6, depending on your preference) have no words. This is very important!

Classical

Listening to classical composers can enhance brain activity and act as a catalyst for improving your health and well-being. The absence of words seems to be the main factor, as songs that contain lyrics have been found to be a distraction when you're trying to focus. I certainly know that if I'm listening to a song with words (especially one that I like), it's not long before I'm singing along. Well, if my mind is focused on the next word to belt out as I practice to become the next rock star, chances are it's not able to focus on the words I need to type, read, or write that are in front of me—at least not as well.

Cinematic

This one was very interesting for me, and I was very excited to listen to my first playlist. My immediate review was, "Wow!" An intense film score can make you feel like you're doing something inspiring or important, even if you're just chipping away at your to-do list. A grandiose, epic soundtrack playing in the background may make even the most mundane task feel like you're changing the world, and thus heightening your concentration and productivity. Cinematic music scores can be empowering, lift your spirits, and brighten your mood. How is it that a movie scene can cause you to burst into tears, or have you on the edge of your seat in a battle scene? The music is scientifically designed to move you in ways you can't do on your own. Try watching one of your favorite scenes in silence; I promise it will not have the same effect.

Video Game

To be clear, I am not a gamer, but this was interesting to me as well, and made a lot of sense. Listening to music composed for video games can be a great tool to help you focus. Every element of a video game is designed to create an enhanced gaming experience for all your senses, and the music can be composed specifically to help you focus on your task without being distracted by its cacophony of sounds. This music generally has no lyrics or human voices, and is barely fast paced to keep you moving forward. Many of these video games involve solving puzzles and dealing with intense situations, so you're subjecting yourself to stimulating and stressful challenges. This is the many hits of dopamine flooding your system as you get the next gold star, unlock the door, or complete the level and get to move on. You feel awesome and want more, so you continue. These musical compositions may be just the thing to propel you onward and keep you zooming through your tasks and your daily to-do list.

Music Between 50 and 80 Beats per Minute

An "alpha state of mind" is what scientists associate with "right brain" activity, or our subjective senses of imagination, creativity, memory, and intuition. When we are awake, we are typically in a state of mind known as "beta," a heightened state of alertness where brain wave activities are between 14 and 30 Hz. When our brain slows to between 7 and 14 Hz, we're in a more relaxed alpha state of mind, which allows us to be more receptive and open, and less critical. The state of mind is what scientists associate with activities that involve our imagination, memory, and intuition, including our "eureka" moments. Listening to music set in the 50 to 80-beat range, puts the brain into an alpha state. Anytime that I'm looking to be creative or tap into my imagination, I'll look for a playlist with music (no words) between 50 and 80 bpm. Physically, I cannot tell you that I "feel" anything in particular, but what I can promise you is that I can get more done, and I feel awesome in the moment when getting the task at hand completed.

Your Favorite Music

When it comes to tackling projects that you're not really excited about, it can help to put music on that you enjoy. Studies have found that putting on your favorite type of music can improve your mood and productivity. The best example I have here is chores around the house. As these items on my to-do list are predominantly reactive (tidying up kids toys/room, dishes, vacuuming, etc.), I'm okay with shutting down my brain (as much as I can) and just enjoying some fun music. The only time this didn't hold true was if the music I listened to was distracting, such as having a beat that's too fast, or lyrics that caught my attention. Another good example I see every day is with construction workers. I don't think I have ever been to a building site where music was not playing. What I wonder is, what if I equipped every person with headphones and the ability to listen to music that improved their focus, productivity, and drive to achieve. What are the possibilities that would improve speed, safety, efficiency, less time off, motivation, and the pure enjoyment of your job?

Thoughts

Our subconscious mind and our thoughts dictate our every move (whether you choose to believe that or not). I heard a saying one time at a conference, which I absolutely loved, and it has to do with all the things we tell ourselves that we MUST do or that we SHOULD have done.

"I must do this today," "I must call that person," "I must get to this place," "I must read about that," and when the time comes and goes because, well, life is life, thoughts are thoughts, and priorities get prioritized, you end up with, "I should have done that today," "I should have called that person," "I should have gone there," and "I should have read more."

So I ask, how many more times in a day are you "MUSTerbating" than "SHOULDing" all over yourself? "Musterbation" is a term coined by famed psychologist Albert Ellis.

It's not easy to take control of your thoughts, but the first step is realizing in that moment what external information you are taking in, what's happening in that moment, and understanding that you absolutely control the outcome.

Randy Taylor is someone I follow, support, and have turned to on many occasions. When it comes to a thought, he says it best:

"There are so few challenges in life that are real. When you truly drill down and discover what it is that negates the great goals in life, you find out it was simply due to the fact that we stopped. We ceased our forward action, that if continued would have brought about the prize in the end. We stop because of a thought."

It normally goes something like this: "I didn't see that coming. I had no idea it would be this hard. I thought I would be so much further by now. This is not working. I give up. I quit." And so it goes. Day after day. Goal after goal. Life after life ends up missing the mark, and it all came down to a thought, a thought that said it was not working. Here is what a thought is: the recall of the storage of information from a past experience that is no longer here, the challenge we encountered, the obstacle we came upon, the setback that was thrust upon is. They are all now in this exact moment from the past. Oh sure, there will be future challenges and difficulties for us all. That's just life, but know the thoughts that pierce your belief are pulled forward from the subconscious mind. This weekend made me think of how easy it is to get sucked down the rabbit hole of despair. This weekend, the weather man (or woman, or whoever wants to take the blame) were oh so wrong again. "Watch for rain coming on holiday Monday," they echoed. Rain? Monday? Really? The only rain drops within a hundred miles were coming from my kids' squirt guns. The forecast no doubt caused far too many to pass on making great plans for the day. By the time the sun began to beat down, it was too late to rally the troops to do whatever ended up being lost. Here's what this all means, I guess: It's wrong, most of the time. I'm not just talking about the weather forecast; I'm speaking of that voice in your head that constantly warns of all the reasons why you can't have what your heart beats for, and what you are so deserving of. Here's all you need to do to remedy that liar inside of your head: When you hear rain, think sun. Have an excellent day.

Relationships

Five Things You May Be Doing to Damage Your Business Relationships

Relationships are hard to build and maintain, and this makes them even more precious. If you've worked hard to establish your business relationships, you need to do everything you can to protect them. However, there are many things you may be doing to ruin these precious relationships, without being aware of it.

Taking Before Giving

Relationships are based on reciprocity. You give and you take. Each party feels that they're getting something valuable from the other side. This is obvious to most business people, but what is the ratio of your giving and taking?

You should never make the other party feel that you're doing something but are expecting something in return. Instead, pay it forward, be overly generous, and wow the other person with all of the value you can, especially in the beginning stages of the relationship.

One-Way Communication

Does it appear to the other person that you talk and never listen? This produces a one-sided relationship that's really not much of a relationship at all. Picture this situation in a personal context and it's easy to see. Most of us avoid people who dominate every conversation in our personal lives.

In a good relationship, there's always a dialog. You should always strive to listen more than you talk. This not only maintains a strong relationship, but you'll also learn a great deal about your partner that you may not have noticed if you were talking.

Secrecy

Secrecy is a major relationship killer. Of course, in business, there are always things that must be kept secret. But you should keep your confidentiality to a minimum. Hiding things makes you appear dishonest, and openness is essential for establishing trust in a relationship.

Try to be as transparent as possible without giving out secrets or too much information. Make sure the other party knows everything they need to know about what's going on. Give the other person plenty of opportunities to ask questions if they need to.

No Rapport

A business relationship is about business, and both parties know it. But if you're all about the business and nothing else, this isn't going to feel much like a relationship, but rather an exchange of commodities.

You need to establish rapport. This means establishing a baseline of comfort on a personal level. Find things that you share in common, and rely on these things to strengthen your bond. When you start by establishing rapport, you create a strong relationship for the long term.

Hard to Say Sorry

Do you have trouble apologizing? This could be damaging your important business relationships. When you do something wrong or make a mistake, own up to it quickly and sincerely. Even major mistakes can be mended if you're willing to apologize. The apology starts you on the path to reconciliation.

Chapter 5

Emotional Drivers

Need for Certainty

Perhaps it's coincidence that as I write this book, we are in the midst of one of the most uncertain times in history: the COVID-19 pandemic. This is by far the most uncertain time I have ever experienced in my life, and the emotional impact it is having, not just on me but on my family, colleagues, and friends, is mind boggling.

Think about the last time you were faced with a situation that you just were not completely certain about—what was your default response? Dive in with no thought? I would be willing to bet, even if you did eventually move forward, it was carefully thought out and calculated, to a point where you felt some sort of certainty. Our brains are hardwired to protect us. Research tells us that our brains are equipped with 5 times the architecture to be able to protect us. Dark forest? Nope! What if an animal attacks you? Bad weather? Nope! Don't drive or travel, because you might get into an accident. Remember, from the section on "fear," that 1600 people, in the wake of 9/11, died due to automobile fatalities because they were too scared to fly. It is the safest form of travel in the world, and yet people decided against it. And in 2018, there were 50 times as many people that died from taking selfies than by shark attacks, and yet we are all scared of sharks. SELFIES!

Our need for certainty is a function of our brains that helps to protect us, such as the decisions we make for our children: where they play, who they play with, where they go to school, and what sports or activities they play. I willingly pawned off my children to daycare when they were 18 months old. On the surface, I effectively gave my child to strangers and said, "See ya!" However, the research I did, the visits, the people I met, and the reviews, were all part of gaining some level of certainty in order for me to make that decision. If I had not taken it upon myself to do those things, chances are my kids would have never gone to daycare. Yet now, they are thriving; they made a very easy transition into school, and are social, loving, caring, active, and creative boys.

What are some things you have done outside of your comfort zone that turned out to be amazing? Traveling somewhere? Dating? Eating a food?

The need for safety, security, reliability, predictability, and known outcomes is all important. Understanding the role of certainty, in these areas in our lives, can definitely protect us.

With that being said, it's also important to recognize that by mindfully releasing your need for certainty (even if it's calculated), it creates more tolerance and patience, as you give up your view as the only way or only option. This in turn can create new opportunities and adventures in your life filled with wonder and happiness.

Need for Variety

Go figure, just when we crave the need for certainty, we also have a dire need for variety: the need for the unknown, the unexpected, to mix things up and keep them interesting. I would argue that just when I do agree that I need variety in my life at the same time, that variety is often calculated. In short, I need some level of certainty in order to incorporate variety. Let me give you an example:

Someone suggests trying a new restaurant or a different kind of food. I immediately think to myself, "Sure." Then I ask what kind of food. Where is it located? Is it busy? How much? All these questions provide some level of certainty so that I can incorporate variety.

In a study, on days when people experienced more variety in their physical surroundings, and were able to spend time in different geographical locations, they were more likely to report feeling "happy," "excited," "strong," and "relaxed" or "attentive." This is amazing to me as I have always recognized that my most productive and fun-filled days were the ones where I seemed to be on the move and, as an extrovert, having multiple interactions throughout the day. What is your variety? Finding your variety in your day will lead to a better you.

"Our results suggest that people feel happier when they have more variety in their daily routines—when they go to novel places and have a wider array of experiences," senior author Catherine Hartley, assistant professor in New York University's Department of Psychology, said in a news release. She added, "The opposite is also likely true: Positive feelings may drive people to seek out these rewarding experiences more frequently."

Need for Significance

The need to feel special or unique in some way is something every human desires. Even those people you know who are "thick" skinned or tough, need to know they are special in some way.

We are social animals and have a deep down burning need for connection. Regardless of your personality type, feeling significant and feeling special to those around you helps you feel safe, is motivating, and can be a driving force in your desire to work toward your goals.

One of the best examples and easiest ways to understand your need for significance is in the workplace and in your relationships.

When you are productive at work, you want to somehow be recognized for your accomplishments, in a way that will motivate you. You are flooded with chemical hormones such as serotonin, oxytocin, and dopamine, and you want more. Your leaders, colleagues, friends, partner, or whoever, might speak about you; your name might show up on a bulletin; you may get a promotion, a new office, a gift, a day off, etc.—just being recognized is the key driver here. Think of the alternative, which we see and hear about every single day: "I hate my job, my boss sucks, and I don't feel like I'm doing anything at work or contributing in any way. As a leader, it's imperative to understand humans if you want to get the most out of your employees. If all you care about is the bottom line and not the people who can help you get there, chances are it's a revolving door. How about in your relationships (or non-relationship)? What makes it great? Does the other person know how much you appreciate them and how they help you? Do you thank them? Do you see them? It's important to understand how you contribute, so that you can be the best partner, friend, parent, sibling, or child. It's not always easy, as everyone has a different "need for significance," but everyone wants to feel special.

Need for Connection

Here is the one time you will hear me absolutely sing the praises of social media. During this pandemic, if it was not for the multitude of platforms that have allowed us to stay in touch with one another, I believe that our problems would far exceed any of the results we have experienced. Your need for love and a feeling of being a part of something is the basic definition of our need for connection. It's called a "culture" in a company for a reason: the word "culture" comes from the Latin "cultus," which means "care." How do you build a company of care? Connecting means "to join, bind, or fasten together." The strength and bond that is formed as a team is stronger than any other force. I played hockey in my previous life, and I have teammates that I have built relationships with that stand true to this day. In fact, because of social media, the 8 other guys from my class at Brown University have stayed in touch since the day we graduated, have all been to each other's weddings, and have since started getting together every couple of years for a reunion. We talk (or chirp) to each other daily, and it's the strongest bond amongst all of us. I would do anything for those guys, and I know that they would do anything for me.

One of my favorite quotes:

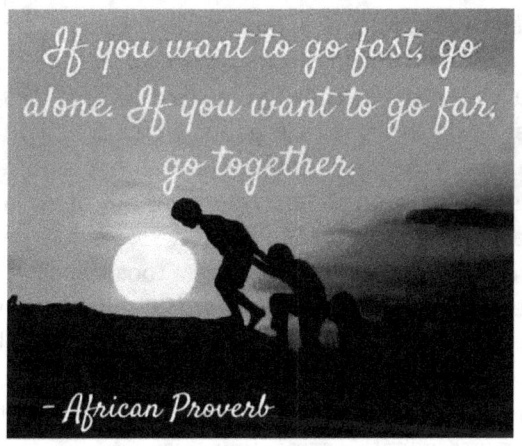

Whether it is family, colleagues, teams, or friends, the stronger the relationship, the stronger the bond, and the further you'll go. The best athletes in the world, regardless of the sport, have a myriad of people in their corner that they trust and rely on. The greatest corporations and most successful people in the world lean on a team of experts to help them.

Through the COVID-19 pandemic, the single biggest lesson that has surfaced, and the single biggest lesson I sincerely believe people have come to realize, is that they want to physically be in front of another human. It's not enough to just talk, text, or video call. We need to embrace one another, shake someone's hand, and sit and enjoy a coffee or a meal while engaging in a face-to-face conversation. I know that people say not to take the little things for granted, and I guess this pandemic has certainly proven that. I have always said that life is not too short but life is extremely valuable. Find a way to connect with people in your life to reinforce and build your bond.

Need for Growth

The need to feel that we are moving forward and/or upward is the primary function of the chemical dopamine. It is widely recommended to write down your goals and check them off as you go. This is because we are visually oriented and need to see that we are making progress. The only way to do this is to have goals. A mistake I'll often see, and that I have done in the past, is making a goal that is outrageous, and then dismissing it as impossible. Remember, our brains are set up to protect us, and will always try and find a way to conserve energy and stop us from doing anything that may seem too difficult. If I said I want you to make 1000 phone calls in 1 year, chances are you would think that number is extremely high, and you would immediately default to figuring out how not to do it. Procrastination is part of the human experience, and we have all done it. The next time you put something off—that is, procrastinate—remember this:

*"Procrastination is like masturbation: in the beginning, it feels good, but in the end, you're just f***ing yourself!"*
~ Michael McCarthy

Now, what if I told you to make 3 calls a day? Simple, right? You can do that in 10 minutes. What will you do for the other 23 hours and 50 minutes? Three calls a day is well over 1000 calls per year. Nailed it!

In sports, players, coaches, teams, and analysts have a strategy called periodization. They break down and look at everything in chunks (i.e. by periods, by quarters, by play, by shift, by pitch, etc.). My experience comes from playing hockey. There are 3 periods in a game. If I got 4–5 shifts per period, at roughly 45–60 seconds per shift, I would be looking at 12–15 total shifts per game, and somewhere between 9 and 15 minutes of total work. It's okay to have one bad shift as long as I don't have 12 or 15 in a row.

In the corporate environment, the most generally adopted metric is quarters (i.e. Q1, Q2, Q3, Q4). What if we looked at taking each quarter and breaking it down into weeks? One year to achieve a goal is a long time away when it's January 1st. You have 12 months to make those 1000 phones calls, and you'll eventually (enter procrastination) get to it. If you look at 12 weeks per quarter, in reality, each "week" is like a month, but it's far less to swallow, and you'll be able to see your goal. A 5-day work week means 4 calls per day and 20 calls per week. That you can do, no problem. Some weeks, you may make 25 calls; and others, you may only make 15. The point here is that you slowly build your confidence, and you are allowing yourself to grow. Understand that each day you achieve a small goal, you get this hit of dopamine and an internal pat on the back, which allows you to move forward and grow. There is a reason why you like being productive. There is a reason why you like to grow. Further to that, if you surround yourself with a team, or share your journey with colleagues or a leader, there are many other benefits.

The secret to being confident is knowing what confidence loves to eat, and then feeding it. The favorite food of confidence is baby steps. Start whatever you fear—do a little, do some more—and your confidence builds. Start, do, do some more, start—the important thing is to take that first step. Bravely overcoming one small fear gives you the courage to take the next step. Whatever it is that you want to get better at, growing feels awesome.

Need for Contribution

The need for contribution is the feeling that we have given something to our family, our friends, or the world.

Make It a Great Day

There are 12 steps in the Alcohol Anonymous program, and research suggests that until the 12th step has been fully adopted, the person in the program has a significant chance or relapsing. The 12th step is "helping other alcoholics."

When you contribute, you connect with the people around you, your colleagues, your friends, your family, society, and the world. When you feel that you have made a difference, you create meaning in your life. Contribution goes beyond just the benefits you will personally gain. By contributing, you connect with the outside world and expand your sense of identity. In North America, when you meet someone new and engage in a candid conversation, the social norm and acceptable first question is, "What do you do?" To which someone will respond with confidence that they are the owner of their company, a lawyer, a doctor, senior c-level executive, professor, professional athlete, teacher, politician … the list can go on and on. If they feel they have contributed or are currently contributing, then it gives them a sense of pride and accomplishment. On the other hand, if someone does not feel that they are contributing in any way, their demeanor and response is far different. They will stumble and tell you that they are thinking about doing this or that, or that they are working toward something or have a plan to do something. In reality, what they are doing can be the most amazing thing, but they do not feel like they are contributing, and that emotional driver is lacking. In Australia, one of the first questions people ask is, "Who are you?" and that sets a totally different stage. If someone asks me what it is that I do, I'm going to go down the path of telling them all about my current work life, my company, and how I used to play hockey. Super! When I think of someone asking me, "Who are you?" or "Who is Jarrett?" a smile immediately appears: "I'm an extremely proud father, I have an amazing wife, and our family is so much fun. We drive each other nuts, and it's the best. I have a warm and beautiful home, I love working out, and my career is amazing. I'm known as the "rainbows and butterflies guy" amongst my friends and colleagues. I love what I do for work, and I can't wait for Mondays. I try every day to make it a great day (some are more challenging than others)." How is that for a much different answer? Now it's easier for my brain to compute that it's not just my job that determines my success or whether or not I have contributed—it's everything in life and around me.

Contribution is a key evolutionary driver that provokes people to help others and is why it is so important.

The tides are slowly turning as the reins are passed down to the next generation. Traditionally, and still predominantly, companies make remarkably little use of this need, working instead on a transactional basis, where the deal is "do as you are told, and you'll get paid." If they could build on the need to contribute, their employees would be far more energized and give much more.

The simplest way to persuade is to ask. When asked for help, many are delighted, as this gives them an opportunity to help. All you need to do in return is to be grateful, and they will be happy to keep on helping you. It also helps build moral, personally or professionally, and best of all, you get far more accomplished (and usually in a shorter time span). Everyone loves to help, and no one knows why. It feels good! Plain and simple. The most successful leaders in any business ask for help from anyone that can. Nowhere is this more evident than in a quote from the late Steve Jobs:

> "It doesn't make sense to hire smart people
> and **tell them** what to do;
> we hire smart people so they can **tell us** what to do."

Part II – Emotional Intelligence

Chapter 6

Emotional Intelligence

What is EI?

"In a study of skills that distinguish star performers in every field from entry-level jobs to executive positions, the single most important factor was not IQ, advanced degrees, or technical experience, it was EQ. Of the competencies required for excellent in performance in the job studies, 67% were emotional competencies."
– Daniel Goleman

As a small business owner or entrepreneur, you know that success is hard to achieve and maintain, no matter what your goal is. It's not enough to be intelligent, or to have the right experience, credentials, or contacts.

Increasingly, it is your "soft skills" that lead to success. But what makes up these soft skills? The answer is emotional intelligence; and unlike IQ, this is something that can be learned. Over the last 20 years, "emotional intelligence" (EI) has become a household word. While many people know what it means generally, the majority don't understand how it impacts their work and daily lives, how to assess and know their own EI, or how to improve EI and the results this improvement might achieve. Everyone is familiar with "intelligence quotient"

(IQ). Most people associate IQ with intelligence, and take for granted that it's something you're born with. Emotional intelligence, which is also called emotional quotient or EQ, is something quite different. Rather than a skill you're born with, it is something you develop by interaction with the people around you.

There is a great deal of research that shows that improving your EI can help you improve in all areas of your business, from sales to management to leadership. Honing and improving your EI will have a positive impact on your personal life as well.

EI is the ability to perceive, control, and evaluate emotions in both yourself and others, individually and in groups. It is a human being's natural ability to understand and interpret emotions. We do this every day without realizing there is a term for it. The idea of emotional intelligence emerged in the early 1990s. The concept was developed by two psychologists and researchers, Peter Salovey and John Mayer, but it became more widely known through Daniel Goleman's 1995 best seller, *Emotional Intelligence: Why It Matters More Than IQ*. Salavoy and Mayer defined emotional intelligence as "the subset of social intelligence that involves the ability to monitor one's own and others' feelings and emotions, to discriminate among them and to use this information to guide one's thinking and actions." What's important is that it involves two separate abilities: 1) The ability to recognize, understand, and manage, and 2) the ability to influence.

In other words, EI allows you to be more self-aware and thus make better decisions. It can also come in handy when selling, persuading co-workers or employees, or solving problems. You can harness your emotions and use them for problem-solving tasks.

EQ counts for twice as much as IQ and technical skills combined, in determining overall success. Your level of EQ has as profound an effect on your ability to perform under pressure. When things are going well in your life, it is imperative to take time out of your day to reflect on what brings you the greatest meaning in your life. Why do you do what you do? If you fail to do this on a regular basis, you risk becoming tranquilized by the trivial, sedated by the small details. Albeit arbitrary, everyone has deadlines and goals they want to achieve. But if you are working toward goals that are not in alignment with your key values and purpose, you face becoming frustrated and cynical when under pressure, losing sight of the reason why you are doing what you are doing.

Why EI Is More Important Than IQ

A growing body of evidence suggests that a quality we've overlooked may be more important than we realize. This quality is emotional intelligence, and many today believe it's more important for business success than IQ.

IQ v. EQ

We all know about IQ. IQ stands for "intelligence quotient," and it is basically a measure of academic intelligence. IQ is determined by your performance on standardized tests with a variety of different tasks.

IQ is very important if you're going to college, but what about in life generally? Emotional intelligence, which is also called emotional quotient (EQ), is your ability to perceive, understand, and regulate emotions. It is therefore the foundation of all people skills or "soft skills."

Finally, EI can be learned, and IQ cannot. Through skills and training, you can improve your emotional intelligence, and this is why it's now playing a key role in business management.

Success in Life

High IQ is no guarantee of success in life. Rather, studies have shown that people with EI are more likely to be successful in both their personal and professional lives. The reason is that IQ helps you solve problems, learn things, reason, and remember details.

But with a high emotional intelligence, you're more self-aware and more in control of your emotions. You're also more empathetic and positive. These are factors that have a greater impact on success than academic intelligence or hard skills.

Emotions drive people. High emotional intelligence is linked with high motivation. People with high EI have a drive that goes beyond the desire for money or title. Their inner motivation pushes them toward achieving their goals.

EI for the Future

One of the reasons why EI research is on the rise today is that it seems to have more relevance to the changing modern business world. IQ helps with innovation, and that's important. But IQ can't solve the major problems the world faces today. In fact, people are more stressed, lonely, and isolated today, in this high-tech world that IQ has given us. IQ also doesn't help us connect with others or build strong relationships.

IQ is far from useless. It helps in many different situations, with logic, problem solving, creativity, and learning new things. But without a strong foundation of EI first, it's impossible for us to realize all that our IQ can help with.

Improving your emotional intelligence can make a major difference in your life, both professionally and personally, by teaching you more about your own emotions and those of the people around you.

www.makeitagreatday.ca

Test Your Emotional Intelligence

*"When awareness is brought to an emotion,
power is brought to your life."*
– Tara Meyer Robson, author

Before you can figure out where you need to focus your attention, you first need to know your current strengths and weaknesses in terms of emotional intelligence. Here are three assessments and activities to help you identify on which areas to focus. You'll create a targeted approach for improving your EI so that you can then apply the strategies you'll learn later.

EI is difficult to measure quantitatively. For this reason, the following exercises will provide information to help you see the big picture of your emotional intelligence, from various different points of view. The actual
Mayor-Salovey-Caruso Emotional Intelligence Test (MSCEIT) costs around $75 to download and use. All of the assessments below are free and available online.

It is essential that you take time to consider each question and answer truthfully. Try to think of examples from the past that you can draw upon. For example, if asked to give a true or false answer for a question such as, "Am I calm in the face of pressure?" give it some thought before hitting the answer button. Think of specific situations and make an informed answer, because the results depend on your honesty and objectivity, and it's not always easy to be honest and objective.

Self-Assessment #1 – Interpersonal Skills Self-Assessment
https://www.skillsyouneed.com/quiz/343479#sthash.d2ROtSGb.dpuf

For your first assessment, you'll complete a questionnaire called the "Interpersonal Skills Self-Assessment." This test is presented by the SkillsYouNeed.com website.

This questionnaire includes sections for four different areas:

- Listening Skills
- Verbal Communication
- Emotional Intelligence
- Working in Groups and Teams

This survey covers not only emotional intelligence but also other soft skills related to EI, such as listening, verbal skills, and the ability to work in teams. As the directions indicate, you need to spend time answering each question, and do so honestly. As it advises, you should compare yourself to those around you if you're unsure how to answer. Once completed, the survey gives you feedback on areas of improvement. In order for the feedback to be accurate and useful, your answers must be as honest as possible.

The questionnaire is free, but you'll need to supply an email address. After you complete the questionnaire, it will give you an overall score as a percentage, as well as a percentage for each category. For each, there will be a small summary and links to further information. It will send a copy of your results to the email you provide. Even answering slowly and considering each answer carefully, the survey takes only a few minutes to complete.

Self-Assessment #2 – *The Maetrix EI Test*
https://globalleadershipfoundation.com/geit/eitest.html

The Maetrix EI test is a similar test that you can try. Each question gives you only two choices, and you have to choose the one that best reflects how you work and think. There are forty questions, and it takes a maximum of 10 minutes to complete.

Once you complete the test, it gives you a score of 1 to 10 in four quadrants: Self-Awareness, Self-Management, Social Awareness, and Relationship Management. There is an explanation of what each of these variants means, underneath your score.

Self-Assessment #3 – *Harvard Business Review (HBR)*
https://hbr.org/2015/06/quiz-yourself-do-you-lead-with-emotional-intelligence

This assessment consists of only 25 questions, to which you rate your answer from "Always" to "Never." The questions revolve around how you handle emotions, how you adapt to change, and soft skills such as leadership or problem solving.

The results you get from the assessment are more detailed than the other two. The test rates you in each of the five EI competencies described above—Self-Awareness, Positive Outlook, Emotional Self-Control, Adaptability, and Empathy—and shows your score visually compared to the overall average of those who have taken the test. It offers explanations and tips on how to improve weak areas.

There's one more component that makes this assessment particularly valuable. It is an optional further exercise. After you take the test, there is a link to download a PDF of the same questions; but rather than a self-assessment, it's an assessment for someone else to complete. You are then supposed to give this PDF to a friend or colleague, with whom you have a close, honest, and caring relationship, to evaluate you. This should lead to a discussion afterward, and there are tips on how to develop this discussion.

With this assessment, you don't only assess yourself based on what you think, but someone who knows you well also gives you feedback.

Chapter 7

Leaders

"When you make people angry, they act in accordance with their baser instincts, often violently and irrationally. When you inspire people, they act in accordance with their higher instincts, sensibly and rationally. Also, anger is transient, whereas inspiration sometimes has a life-long effect."
– Peace Pilgrim

Use EI to enhance leadership and people management skills. The same concepts of emotional intelligence are important for dealing with staff, outsourced employees, and contractors.

Numerous studies have looked at the financial implications of emotional intelligence in leadership. These studies show that high EI leaders produce better results overall. One particular study looked at 186 corporate executives and found that companies led by high EI individuals were more likely to be profitable.

Other studies have found that executives spend 45 percent of their day listening. However, as much as 95% of these executives have never taken a course in how to listen effectively. You can easily imagine what would happen if this overwhelming majority of executives in leadership roles could sharpen their emotional intelligence.

One of the major challenges in company leadership in relation to EI is the generation gap. For the older generation, who are now, for the most part, in management positions, emotional intelligence and soft skills were not considered important. Rather, the importance of hard skills was stressed.

Younger workers, on the other hand, want more than just a paycheck. They want to better themselves, and they seek fulfillment through work, not just money or a high position. They have to thrive in a modern work environment, where emotional intelligence is essential.

EI matters in management because a manager with high emotional intelligence can create a positive work environment, which leads to increased revenue and growth. They know how to respond to their employees' needs, they listen to their employees, and they can easily diffuse tense or stressful situations appropriately (not just with fake positivity). A highly emotionally intelligent manager can balance focusing on himself/herself, with focusing on his/her staff, and focusing on the wider world.

How to Develop EI for Leaders

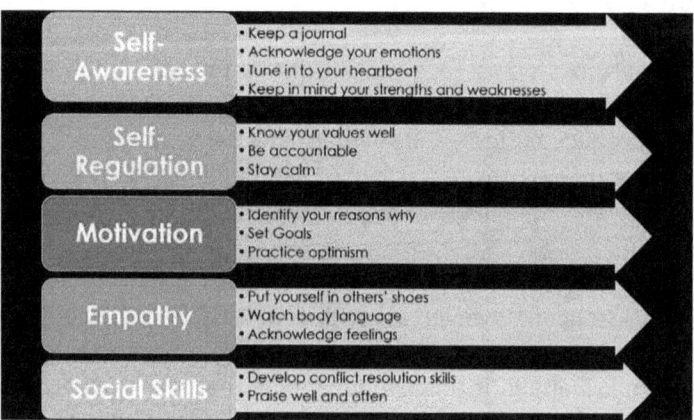

Self-Awareness	• Keep a journal • Acknowledge your emotions • Tune in to your heartbeat • Keep in mind your strengths and weaknesses
Self-Regulation	• Know your values well • Be accountable • Stay calm
Motivation	• Identify your reasons why • Set Goals • Practice optimism
Empathy	• Put yourself in others' shoes • Watch body language • Acknowledge feelings
Social Skills	• Develop conflict resolution skills • Praise well and often

Self-Awareness

People who have a healthy sense of self-awareness are what you might call "comfortable in their own skin." They maintain a good understanding of their own emotions and how their emotions impact those around them. Self-awareness usually includes a healthy level of self-confidence and an ability to laugh at oneself.

Self-Regulation

In addition to understanding their own emotions, people who are emotionally intelligent can demonstrate maturity and restraint when revealing them. They don't suppress or repress emotions, but employ judgment and control when expressing them. They think before acting, and they are open to change.

Motivation

Emotionally intelligent people are generally optimistic and are driven by inner motivation, rather than by a desire for money, titles, or social acceptance. They have an inner resilience that makes it hard to shake their confidence. Failure is not a big deal to EI people.

Empathy

Strong emotional intelligence comes with a high degree of compassion and understanding of human nature. People with high EI find it easy to connect emotionally with others. This is why EI is important for business; it translates to stellar customer service and excellent "soft skills" or people skills.

Social Skills

Emotionally intelligent people are widely respected by those they know and work with. They generally like people, and they can quickly build rapport and trust that is genuine. They don't like "playing games" with people. They also build relationships and personal networks well.

The 5 Pillars of Emotional Intelligence

Self-Awareness	Self-Regulation	Motivation	Empathy	Social Skills
They maintain a good understanding of their own emotions and how they represent them	They don't suppress or repress emotion, but employ judgment and control when expressing them	They are generally optimistic and are driven by inner motivation, rather than a desire for money, titles or social acceptance.	Strong emotional intelligence comes with a high degree of compassion and understanding of human nature.	They generally like people and they can quickly build rapport and trust that is genuine.

After reading the above, you may get the idea that emotional intelligence is simply unbounded positivity. You may think that an emotionally intelligent individual is one who is always agreeable, optimistic, happy, calm, and motivated. This, however, isn't the case at all, because these are personality traits.

For example, there may be an individual with an extremely low EI, who is also positive and constantly happy. Think of a person you know who is always positive but seems totally unaware of the feelings of others, or who represses all of their negative feelings. You may have a manager, for example, with low EI, who turns a blind eye to problems, or refuses to deal with sensitive issues because he or she wants to be positive all the time.

On the other hand, a person with high EI may face extremely tough challenges because they know it's the right thing to do. In this situation, they may not be calm, happy, or positive. But their inner resolve and their emotional awareness tell them it's the right thing to do.

In the example of the person who is not emotionally intelligent but simply positive, consider anger. It isn't healthy to fly off the handle and go into a rage, but it's also not healthy to act passive-aggressively. The manager described above would try to bury his or her anger, which may lead to the problem not being handled, or cause other adverse effects. A person with a high level of EI would, although angry, talk directly and in a controlled way to the concerned parties so that the problem can be resolved quickly and appropriately.

Finally, those with high EI can handle constructive criticism and feedback. Because they are emotionally open, they don't feel the sting of criticism. With their emotions well controlled, they know that criticism is feedback that leads to better performance as a result. On the other hand, those with low EI blame others and feel victimized. They become defensive when they feel they're under attack.

One common myth related to EI is that women are more emotionally intelligent than men. While it may be true that women tend to be more empathetic and in touch with their emotions than men, EI actually has nothing to do with gender.

For example, men tend to be conditioned to be more self-confident and better at handling stress, which are also traits of highly emotionally intelligent people. The point is that anyone can improve their emotional intelligence, irrespective of gender, age, race, or background.

EQ and IQ

There are two important points to keep in mind regarding EI (EQ) and IQ. First, there is no correlation between IQ and EQ. Remember that your IQ level is something you're born with. EQ, on the other hand, can be developed. IQ is static, but EQ is fluid, like a skill that can be learned through study and training.

A person with a high IQ can have a low EQ. Consider a researcher who spends his or her days in a laboratory, brilliantly unlocking the secrets of the universe, but who can't maintain relationships. On the other hand, a person with a high EQ does not necessarily need to be intelligent in other ways. Imagine someone you know without a great deal of "book smarts" but who seems to really know and understand people well.

Why EI Matters

EI is vitally important to your career or business, no matter what you do. Everyone knows how important "soft skills" are. Good soft skills are just one aspect or expression of a high level of emotional intelligence.

Just consider this case study. Chris is a bank manager who, to all outward appearances, has everything going for him. He has an MBA, plenty of energy and enthusiasm, charisma, and a great sense of humor. Yet despite having all of the right ingredients, his career is falling apart. Turnover in his department is high, and morale is low.

Chris has a high IQ but a low EI. He has all of the hard skills necessary to excel at his job, but his lack of EI is ruining him. He makes sarcastic comments and jokes that destroy his employees' morale, without him realizing it. Whenever questioned or criticized, he becomes defensive and quits listening. And any sensitive or difficult issue with his staff that he's not comfortable with, he ignores.

While IQ can get you in the door, you need EI in order to thrive. Goleman conducted research, looking at 500 worldwide organizations, and he found that people who scored the highest EI rose to the top. According to Goleman, "EI matters twice as much as the technical and analytic skills combined for start performance. The higher people move up in the company, the more crucial EI becomes."

Currently, the economy is changing in such a way that EI is becoming increasingly important. The shift from manufacturing to tech and service jobs means that different skills are needed. Critical thinking, problem solving, and good communication are increasingly important. These changes make EI more important than ever.

Strong EI can help with leadership, retention of staff, sales, and growing your business. Improving EI will also lead to improvements in your personal life. You'll be better able to handle stress, maintain important relationships, listen, empathize, and control your own emotions and express them in a healthy way.

Self-Awareness

Leaders who are self-aware make better decisions, are more authentic, and come across to others with more genuine humility. A leader should be like this, rather than being arrogant or unconcerned with the feelings of others.

Keep a Journal

Spend a few minutes each day writing down your thoughts. Don't think too much about what to write; rather, let the pen move across the page. Try to write down your thoughts as honestly as possible, as quickly as they pop into your mind. Go back sometimes and read past entries. This helps you formulate your thoughts and get to know your feelings better.

Acknowledge Your Emotions

Emotionally intelligent people don't suppress or deny the feelings they're having, even when they're uncomfortable. When you experience strong emotions, take the time to fully experience them. When angry, let yourself be angry. When in the heat of the moment with strong emotions, look back and try to examine why you're feeling them. What triggered or pre-empted those feelings?

Tune in to Your Heartbeat

Your heartbeat tells you a great deal about where you are emotionally. Can you tune into or connect to the sound of your own beating heart? How well you can sense your heartbeat is an interesting way to measure how self-aware you are.

Remember Your Strengths and Weaknesses

Examine yourself carefully to discover your natural strengths and weaknesses. Although you naturally want to improve your weaknesses, it's important to know exactly what they are. This will help you better understand how to handle a situation. You'll know when you need to reach out to someone else for help.

Self-Regulation

Leaders who know how to regulate themselves don't compromise their values, make rushed decisions, or attack others.

Know Your Values Well

What is your code of ethics? Do you have a clear idea of what you will not compromise? What are the values that you live by? Think about the times you felt happiest or most fulfilled. When you consider the reasons for this fulfilled feeling, you can easily discover your most important values. Keep these values in mind at all times. This will keep you from compromising or making a decision that goes against them.

Be Accountable

Whenever anything goes wrong, take the responsibility for it yourself. Even if it was clearly someone else's fault, try to see if there is anything you could have done better to prevent it. If one of your employees makes a mistake, for example, tell yourself that you could have trained them better. The purpose is not to beat up on yourself and your abilities, but rather to get you into the habit of not blaming others. When you do something wrong, admit your mistake and face the consequences fully.

Stay Calm

What are the emotions or situations that trigger strong emotions for you? Identify them and make a plan for dealing with them calmly, even if it means just taking a moment to breathe and get centered when a difficult situation arises. In your free time, practice meditation, deep breathing, or another stress reduction technique that you can use when you need it.

Motivation

Self-motivated leaders work toward their goals and have high standards for the work they do.

Identify Your Reasons Why

Take a look at your current career and position, and ask yourself what reasons brought you to it. If you're happy with your present working status, try to discover what drove you to reach it. If you're unhappy with things in general, try to find the root of the problem or find a new way to look at your career; for example, you might currently be in transition moving toward a goal.

Set Goals

If you haven't already, set some goals to help you stay motivated. Choose a few annual goals for your work. Ask yourself what you'd like to be doing this time next year. Try to be as specific as possible; for example, name a specific position or dollar amount. Keep these goals in mind. You may also set personal goals or other types of goals too.

Practice Optimism

True optimism isn't about being blindly positive all of the time. Real optimists find the good in things, even when things are generally not good. They see the silver lining, and this helps them maintain balance when
adversity strikes. Even when something terrible happens, try to find the positive in it, and focus on this positive instead of the negative.

Empathy

There are three types of empathy:

Cognitive Empathy – Cognitive empathy is the ability to understand another person's perspective. When a leader understands the other person's perspective, they can communicate and express themselves better to that other person. You can communicate in a way that will be meaningful to the other person.

Emotional Empathy – This is what we usually mean by the word "empathy." It is the ability to feel what someone else feels. This is very important when mentoring, training employees, managing clients, reading group dynamics, or helping staff members through difficulties.

Empathic Concern – Empathic concern is the ability to sense what another person needs from you, even when they don't come out and say it. This is another tool to help facilitate better communication.

To improve your empathy, you can practice the following.

Put Yourself in Others' Shoes

At every opportunity, put yourself in someone else's shoes. Take the time to look at situations from other people's perspectives. With practice, you'll be able to understand others much better, and this skill will greatly improve your interpersonal skills. You'll be much better at understanding your employees and partners.

Watch Body Language

Pay attention to your body language and what emotions it expresses to others. If your body language isn't expressing what you want it to, consciously try to change your body language. Also pay attention to the body language of others.

Acknowledge Feelings

When someone shares a feeling with you, acknowledge it. One way to do this is to try to explain the feeling to them or reword what they say to express the emotion underneath. "Explain the feeling" doesn't mean telling someone else how they feel. It means giving words to the feeling, and confirming that you understand.

For example, if an employee loses a good potential client, and they say, "I am frustrated that I couldn't secure that contract," you could say something like, "You really wanted that to be a major achievement, didn't you?" This either confirms the feeling or asks the other person to clarify further.

Social Skills

Develop Conflict Resolution Skills

Embrace conflict and learn conflict resolution skills. Conflict is inevitable, and it needs to be handled as soon as possible. It arises out of a clash of differing needs. Healthy conflict resolution involves understanding the feelings and perspectives of others, and calmly reaching a compromise or agreement that will satisfy the different needs of the parties involved. Study conflict resolution, and take training courses if available.

Praise Well and Often

Praise your staff regularly, and make sure they understand that they are valued by you. Make sure that you always offer praise along with criticism when criticism is necessary. If your employees understand that they are valued by you, they will be better able to handle this criticism, and they'll be more confident and motivated in their work.

9 Tips for Managing People Using EI

- **One on Ones**. Take time to regularly speak with your staff one on one. This will help you better understand who they are, and you'll then be able to help them achieve their goals. At the very least, schedule a quick 30-minute touch-point meeting with each of your staff bi-weekly, or more if it's possible.

- **Reward Your Staff**. Get into a regular routine of rewarding your staff for each of their achievements. Make this a regular part of your organization's operations. This will provide your staff with plenty of praise and positivity.

- **Establish a Balance to Prevent Burnout.** You can keep morale up by balancing out each member's workload. As part of your job as manager, try to lighten each member's load and make it easier for them as much as possible, rather than piling on more work. Burnout is a major issue, not only for productivity but for workers' emotional well-being.

- **Make Work Fun.** Try to create a workplace that is as fun as possible. This will help you attract and keep good employees, while also creating a good corporate culture where EI is in full effect. There are many ways to do this. One is to give employees more control over their daily work lives. Let them come up with and test their own ideas. Give them creative space to work in, and offer plenty of fun challenges. You can also gamify tasks and office operations.

- **Be Transparent.** Don't hide things from your employees. Make sure they understand all of the information they need to know, and answer their questions or concerns. Don't "hide behind the title." The more they feel that you're being transparent with them, the better they'll be able to communicate with you.

- **Convey Your Mission.** Clearly convey your mission to your employees, and help them understand it. Remind them from time to time, and make sure that they keep it in mind as they go about their daily tasks. With the mission in mind, a staff member will know what to do when a difficult situation arises, because they'll be looking at the big picture.

- **Keep Staff Up to Date.** Hold regular group meetings to go over what's coming up in the coming weeks, months, and years. Always keep your staff abreast of what is going to happen in the near future. Make sure they understand how your immediate and future plans align with your mission and vision.

- **Encourage Unity**. Create a great team with your staff. Create situations where your staff will collaborate and cooperate, rather than compete. Communication and collaboration are the keys to success in today's economy, and people flourish when they're working together as a group toward a common goal.

- **Give Your Staff Leadership Opportunities**. Rather than managing in a top-down way, give your staff members opportunities to be leaders. Create situations and encourage them to take the lead, share opinions, make decisions, and have a say in their work.

Chapter 8

Sales

Concepts to Increase Sales

> *"Emotional competence is the single most important personal quality that each of us must develop and access to experience a breakthrough. Only through managing our emotions can we access our intellect and our technical competence. An emotionally competent person performs better under pressure."*
> – Dave Lennick, Executive VP,
> American Express Financial Advisers

Learn how EI can drive sales performance so that you can apply it to your business and increase your sales and conversions.

Soft skills are critical to sales success. In fact, they're more important than hard skills or technical skills. This is borne out by a 2013 study by Millennial Branding and American Express, which found that over 60% of managers felt that soft skills are the most important ones found in new hires.

Why are soft skills so critically important in sales? The reason is that you need to understand the customer's emotions and make decisions based on their emotions on the fly. Buying is an emotional process, and you need to understand, predict, and guide the buyer's emotions. You need to know not only what the customer is feeling but why they are feeling it.

Emotional intelligence is important, not only in building relationships with your customers but also internally. It's what drives your sales team to do their best. What this means is that your emotional intelligence, and that of your sales staff, has a direct result on your sales performance.

Case studies abound showing that salespeople with high EI outsell those with low EI. They also show that staff, hired or developed for EI, show an increase in client satisfaction and retention, and higher sales figures for the company.

To take just one example, AMEX gave EI training to half of its financial advisors. The following year, the group that had received EI training increased its sales by 18.1%, while the untrained group increased by only 16.2%.

In a sales situation, a person with a low EI may let their emotions get the best of them. He or she may become nervous and tongue-tied, may sweat excessively, and talk too much. Without the skills to understand the customer's emotional situation, they may avoid negotiations, offer discounts too quickly, or oversell. They won't be able to receive the clues from the customer, telling them what the customer wants or that the customer is ready to buy.

Without strong EI skills, the salesperson may not handle a customer's rejection well. Due to lack of confidence, they may play it safe and settle for a lower price than they should have. They might offer a discount in order to avoid negotiation, which stresses them out.

This salesperson needs to improve their EI so that they:

- Can read and understand customer emotions, and grasp underlying reasons for these emotions.
- Negotiate appropriately with confidence and with the best interests of both the customer and company in mind.
- Can deal with the sometimes uncomfortable situations that arise during the negotiation process, and be able to think fast and maintain composure when things aren't going well.
- Can handle sudden changes or unexpected things that come about during the course of the sales process.

On the other hand, a salesperson with a high EI can stay cool and calm in a difficult situation. They can offer the appropriate solution to problems.

They're confident and motivated to make the sale, both for the company and the customer. They listen, read the customer's emotions, and react with empathy. They can control their own emotions while maintaining a big picture view of what's best for all parties involved. Their confidence allows them to stay in control of the negotiation process. The salesperson will also be able to handle rejection if the sale doesn't go as planned.

On the following page is a summary of how your EI affects your sales performance in each of the competencies originally identified by Goleman.

Self-Awareness

- Salespeople with high EI are confident and can easily gain the trust of customers. They seem authentic and take responsibility when the sale doesn't go down as planned.
- Salespeople with low EI are less likeable and seem insincere. They are likely to be defensive and to put the customer on the defensive.

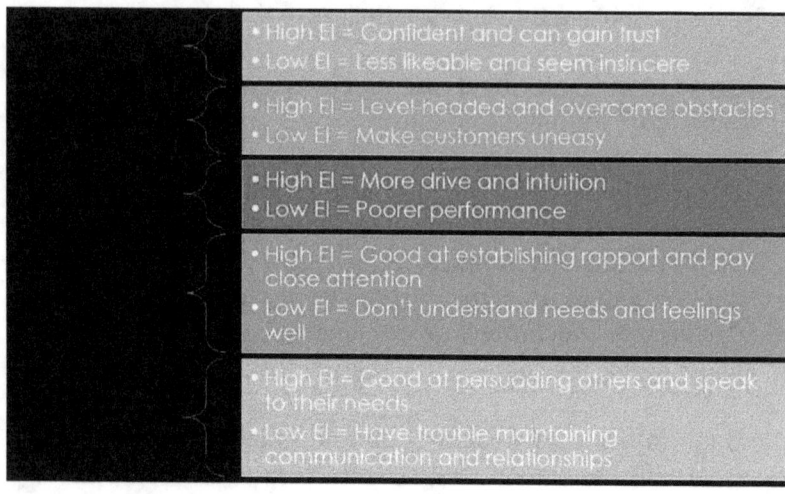

Self-Regulation

- Salespeople with high EI are level-headed during the sales process, and overcome obstacles easily.
- Salespeople with low EI make customers uneasy often, by making things tense or because they come off as immature or unpredictable.

Motivation

- Highly EI salespeople have more drive and initiative than other salespeople, and are always looking for the next opportunity. They seem as if they want to close the sale for some inner reason, and not just for the the commission or promotion.
- Salespeople with low EI generally perform poorly, and this is often obvious to customers.

Empathy

- Salespeople with high EI are good at establishing rapport. They pay attention and listen closely when the customer is talking. They put themselves in the customer's shoes and can adapt to any communication style.
- Salespeople with low EI don't understand the customer's feelings and needs well, and often don't care. It's hard for them to establish a good relationship with the customer.

Social Skills

- Salespeople with high EI are good at persuading others and speaking directly to their needs. They know how to keep communication open and flowing, and can build strong relationships easily.
- Salespeople with low EI have trouble maintaining communication and relationships. They relate to people on a somewhat shallow level.

How to Increase Your EI for Sales

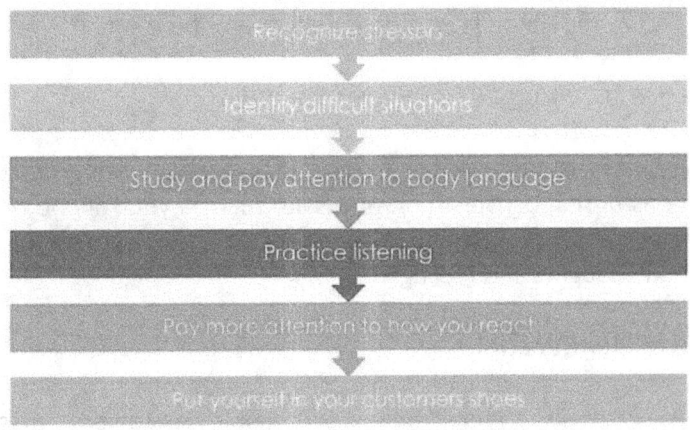

Identify Your Stress Triggers

Recognize what stresses you and how it makes you feel. Learn your specific stress triggers and how you react to them. Develop a plan for reacting in a way that is calm and collected. Put this plan into action, and if it doesn't work, try to think of something else until you find something that does work.

Identify Your Difficult Situations

As with stress triggers, create a plan for how you can handle these situations better. Difficult situations are a part of life, and especially sales. Examples include tough prospects, customer complaints, "putting out fires," and other complex situations. Your reaction can be controlled by learning better self-awareness.

Study Body Language

Study and pay attention to other people's body language, facial expressions, and non-verbal signals. What underlying emotions or thoughts does this non-verbal communication convey? Simply paying more attention to what's not said in a conversation or sale can help you better understand the other person's emotions.

Practice Listening

In conversation, spend more time listening than talking. Avoid distractions during conversation or a sale, such as your phone or text messages. Practice focusing solely on the person talking to you, and on their thoughts and feelings.

Watch Your Reactions

Pay attention to how you react to people. Try to see yourself as another person would see you. How do you greet other people? How do you initiate or wrap-up conversation? Are you happy with the way you do these things, or could you improve? Write down how you could improve, and practice.

Put Yourself in their Shoes

Try as much as possible to put yourself in the shoes of your customer. Consider the sale through the eyes of your prospect. Try to understand what roles and responsibilities they may be juggling, or what problem they're trying to solve. Ask yourself how you can make their life easier. This will help you improve your empathy.

The above tips involve a great deal of self-reflection. In order to improve your EI for sales, you should put aside a little time each day, or as much as possible, for this self-reflection. During this scheduled time, your only concern is improving your EI. Treat it as if it were a task required for work, and give it whatever time you can, even if it's only minutes per day.

During this time, go back over the latest encounters with prospects, and ask yourself questions like:

- What did I do well today, and how can I repeat that?
- Why did I react the way I did to a prospect or customer?
- What would have been a better response during the sales meeting?
- What did I do wrong today, and how can I avoid repeating that?
- Who can I ask for help, mentoring, coaching, or advice?

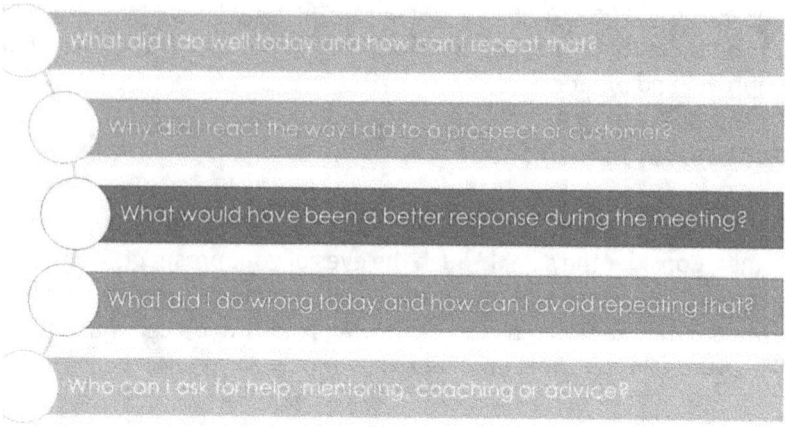

- What did I do well today and how can I repeat that?
- Why did I react the way I did to a prospect or customer?
- What would have been a better response during the meeting?
- What did I do wrong today and how can I avoid repeating that?
- Who can I ask for help, mentoring, coaching or advice?

EI Traits to Look for When Hiring Sales Staff

You should also use EI for hiring your sales staff. Look for salespeople that have a high level of emotional intelligence in each of the five key areas.

Self-Awareness:

- Does the candidate understand their own strengths or weaknesses?
- Can the candidate handle constructive criticism?
- Does the candidate stay calm when faced with difficulty or a stressful situation?

Self-Regulation:

- Can the candidate convey their emotions in a way that is effective and appropriate?
- Is the candidate adept at expressing difficult emotions, such as disagreement or anger?

Motivation:

- Is the candidate driven by a desire for success or personal reasons, other than just the desire for money or title?
- Does the candidate truly strive to improve himself/herself and do their best?
- Is the candidate generally optimistic and confident?
- In a problem-solving situation, does the candidate try to solve the problem quickly, or dwell on the negative?

Empathy:

- Does the candidate act with empathy and understanding?
- Does the candidate feel it's their responsibility to satisfy the customer and meet their needs?

Social Skills:

- Can the candidate quickly establish rapport and build trust?
- Is the candidate generally likeable?
- Does the candidate respect those around them?
- Is the candidate respected by those around them?

What next:

1. Select at least 3 EI strategies and techniques to apply to help boost your sales.
2. Complete the "downtime exercises" this week, or after you've had a sales situation. What did you learn about yourself?
3. If you have sales people working for you, list at least 3 ways you can help support and improve their EI.
4. Have your sales people complete the assessments presented earlier. Based on the results, have them identify their key areas of strength, and work to further refine these. Explain to them that although they may feel compelled to work on their weaknesses, it is actually much easier to focus on developing their strengths. Pick 2–3 strengths and have them work toward improving these.

www.ingramcontent.com/pod-product-compliance
Lightning Source LLC
Chambersburg PA
CBHW070922080526
44589CB00013B/1402